MONMOUTH COUNTY
HISTORIC
LANDMARKS

MONMOUTH COUNTY
HISTORIC
LANDMARKS

RANDALL GABRIELAN

Charleston  London

THE
History
PRESS

Published by The History Press
Charleston, SC 29403
www.historypress.net

All images are courtesy of the author unless otherwise noted.

First published 2011

Manufactured in the United States

ISBN 978.1.60949.240.3

Library of Congress Cataloging-in-Publication Data

Gabrielan, Randall
Monmouth County Historic landmarks / Randall Gabrielan.
p. cm.
ISBN 978-1-60949-240-3
1. Historic sites--New Jersey--Monmouth County. 2. Historic buildings--New Jersey-
-Monmouth County. 3. Monuments--New Jersey--Monmouth County. 4. Historical
museums--New Jersey--Monmouth County. 5. Monmouth County (N.J.)--History, Local. 6.
Monmouth County (N.J.)--Biography. I. Title.
F142.M7G33 2011
974.9'46--dc23
2011019691

Contents

CONTENTS

CONTENTS

HOW TO USE THIS BOOK

This book, organized by municipality, is divided into four chapters, a number chosen to provide a reasonable organizational split, while avoiding many small ones. Listed sites are those that are available to the public as determined by various criteria, which include regular admission of the public for exhibition purposes, access of the public for events of varied kind and frequency and open presence on or as public streets and open for worship. Several churches are included, and others not herein likely also qualify; standards for a "historic site" are and should be informal, flexible and receptive to our changing perspective of what is important and should be preserved. No private residences are part of the volume by design, even if they could meet the "prominent street presence" criterion. Private residences are present in each of the historic districts herein, so it is incumbent upon district visitors to respect privacy rights.

The book deliberately omits a map, considering the reality of easy access to online mapping services and a growing use of GPS devices. To facilitate both of these direction-finding aids, addresses for each location are listed for each entry to assist the navigational aid. The author also notes the continued utility and convenience of large-scale county maps published by Hagstrom and others.

Open hours at publication are given where known and believed reliable. However, some may change during the shelf life of this book, notably by smaller organizations coping with the usual challenges faced by small, often volunteer groups. Thus it may benefit readers to check before visiting, so websites and telephone numbers are given when available and known. A number of sites are houses of worship, reflecting that historical churches are public monuments by virtue of the importance of religion in American life. The author believes that the best way to see a house of worship is to experience it during its intended purpose, admittedly not always convenient for a variety of reasons. Several churches herein are participants in the described self-guided tour. In addition, all are prominent on the street.

The term "events" is a catchall that may include the organization's regular meetings as well as special happenings, which one expects may be advertized to the public. The abbreviation "WOM" refers to the site's participation at publication in a self-guided tour on the first weekend in May organized by the Monmouth County Historical Commission, an event during which these sites are open for extended hours.

The other extensively used abbreviation "NRHP," preceding a year, reflects the date the place was entered on the National Register of Historic Places. Please note that the contact information provided at the end of each entry refers to the main site and not to any ancillary place mentioned at the end of some pieces to provide regional context or inform of another nearby places of interest.

This book intends to embrace all major historic sites open to the public, a good representation of Monmouth's historic houses of worship and museums relating to the history of Monmouth County. Subjectivity enters any such selection process, and the author acknowledges that "major" is not an objective criterion. Space constraints also influenced choices. The author assumes personal responsibility for the selection process; thus, if a reader believes that a certain omitted site should have been included because a comparable one is herein, the author's judgment prevailed.

DISCLOSURE: the author is employed by the County of Monmouth as the executive director of its historical commission. The work was researched and written as a private project. The observations are strictly his own and are not to be imputed to the County, any of his associates there or any representative of a site described herein.

INTRODUCTION

"M onmouth is a very historic county"—a truism hardly needed to be voiced among the initiated—runs the risk of falling into a cliché if the places that reflect, exhibit and honor the county's rich history are not cared for. The greatest need of historic sites is money because their preservation and operation are costly. Everyone may not be able to donate, but all can and should back a fiscal environment to enable the stewards of our shared heritage to survive and prosper. Such an environment includes adequate financial support by public entities, especially the ones that own historic properties. Support should also embrace favorable tax treatment for tax-paying private citizens who own historic properties and bear the higher costs of maintaining properties that improve our communities for the benefit of all.

The easiest form of public support is the presence of visitors to the sites and their voices as advocates when public policy issues emerge. The author's long experience in support of historic sites via research, advocacy, publicity and the operational assistance of one makes it apparent that many more citizens claim interest in historic sites than actually go to them. However, when the reluctant visitor is led to these sites he often enjoys the experience and wonders why he did not visit earlier. This book intends to encourage visitation and to make the experience easier. It is the broadest and deepest known compilation of Monmouth County historic sites, tells why they are important and offers guidelines for their visitation. For practical purposes, the book is an invitation to look and see. Many listed sites have regional suggestions to facilitate seeing or studying nearby related places. Indeed, this book is a local aid and reinforcement of key goal number two of the 2011–16 *New Jersey Historic Preservation Plan*, which aims to "expand understanding and appreciation of history and historic preservation among New Jersey citizens, elected officials, students and organizations across the State."

CHAPTER 1

BAYSHORE REGION

ATLANTIC HIGHLANDS

Strauss Mansion Museum
Atlantic Highlands Historical Society
27 Prospect Circle (at corner of Mount Avenue)
Atlantic Highlands, NJ 07716

Adolph Strauss, a wealthy New York importer and merchant, built this summer home in 1893, located near the highest point of the borough's hill section, a region dotted with numerous Shingle- and Queen Anne–style houses of the period. This section and these houses give the borough its most familiar and best-preserved physical characteristic. Strauss's house is distinguished as the only Queen Anne–style house museum open to the public in Monmouth County.

Atlantic Highlands enjoyed a quarter century of rapid expansion that followed the construction of a modest pier in 1879, one expanded shortly thereafter and replaced in 1892 by the Central Railroad of New Jersey, which was then compelled to relocate its shore dock from Sandy Hook. The town acquired a distinct Methodist character in 1881 when the Reverend James E. Lake prompted the purchase of four hundred acres to form the Atlantic Highlands Association, an organization that aimed to sell lots and establish a Methodist resort. The association's large-scale map of numbered lots is still remarkably useful in tracing house history in Atlantic Highlands.

The Strauss Mansion dominance over its surroundings stems from its standing as perhaps the town's tallest building while also located near its highest spot.

The church's attempt to establish governance over the land was defeated in court; the case is background to the formation of a borough in 1887.

Solomon D. Cohen, New York architect, designed Strauss's two-and-a-half-story house, built on association lot number 997. No image of the place as built is known to exist, but the house, expanded in 1896 and altered numerous times, in time reached twenty-one rooms. Strauss was there for little more than a decade. His former residence, which declined in modern times, suffered the indignity of use as a rooming house and as the set of a horror movie. Its condition was horrific indeed when acquired in 1981 by the Atlantic Highlands Historical Society for adaptive use.

The society undertook an ongoing preservation project that, through three decades' persistence, has resulted in a room-by-room restoration. The house, which first opened to the public in 1986, combines functions that show some rooms with Victorian-era furnishings while giving over others to history exhibits and a library. Thus the visitor can gain an insight into life at the mansion's origins and history of the region over the centuries, including the pre-European settlement period, while accessing a reference library. Once known as The Towers, the tall building on a high elevation also offers splendid views of its environs.

www.atlantichighlandshistory.org; 732.291.1861
Access: Sunday hours in season; events; WOM. Parking: street.

HIGHLANDS

Twin Lights State Historic Site (NRHP 1970)
198 Lighthouse Road
Highlands, NJ 07732

Twin Lights is nationally known as a lighthouse architectural masterpiece, but it also contains a museum with an informative exhibition on both lighthouses and lifesaving and has served as a site of scientific discovery.

The Navesink Light Attendants Station is the official name for one of America's most striking lighthouses, the one widely known as Twin Lights for the dual lamps that were a fundamental element to the facility's establishment in 1828. The light's erection high in the Highlands of the Navesink was planned to provide mariners a longer-distance awareness of their approach to land, while the second light was intended to distinguish this lighthouse from the ground-level light at Sandy Hook. The original blue split-stone structures were identical but not durable and were replaced by the present Romanesque-style towers that are connected at grade by a building that housed keepers' quarters. Visitors may notice that architect Joseph Lederle's design, built in 1862, embraced asymmetrical towers: one

Careful observers will notice that the square and hexagonal towers may disqualify these lights as true twins, but their predecessors were identical.

square, the other hexagonal. Their lack of uniformity has puzzled observers since the distinction was first noticed.

The significance of Twin Lights to the Lighthouse Service may be inferred from its regular position in the employment of technological advances. One of the most significant improvements was the 1841 installation of the first Fresnel lenses in the United States. This lens was an innovation developed in France which employs a series of prisms that creates the effect of expanding the projection of light from its source. In 1898, a later Fresnel lens, a nine-foot-wide bivalve illuminated by a carbon-arc light, cast a beam visible twenty-two miles away. Twin Lights was the first major seacoast lighthouse to have its own generating plant. Exhibited inside this brick building located behind the lighthouse is the Fresnel lens that was formerly in the south tower. A frame building near the entrance on the north is a former lifesaving structure. The lighthouse was decommissioned in 1949 and acquired by the State of New Jersey in 1962. A light remains in the north tower, which is illuminated for exhibition purposes. That tower can be climbed by visitors.

In 1899, inventor Guglielmo Marconi made the first successful demonstration of the ship-to-shore wireless telegraph at this site. Its elevation over the sea also made the spot an effective place for the early testing of radar.

While the lighthouse is the main event at Twin Lights, the structure also contains a museum that displays an effective, well-designed and annotated exhibition on lifesaving and lighthouses. The view from both the tower and grounds often places the repeat visitor in a regular state of awe. Twin Lights was designated a National Historic Landmark in 2006.

www.twin-lights.org; 732.872.1814
Access: seven days a week in summer, Wednesday through Sunday in winter; WOM. Parking: lot.

HOLMDEL

Dr. Robert W. Cooke's Medical Office (NRHP 2011)
67 McCampbell Road
Holmdel, NJ 07733

Dr. Cooke's medical office is significant as the oldest known stand-alone physician's building in New Jersey and is surely one of the oldest—perhaps

The inauspicious exterior of Dr. Cooke's medical office obscures the experience one can feel while inside, that of entering a space where medical practice was primitive.

the oldest—in the country. The small, inauspicious, vernacular building possesses an interior ambiance that suggests to the visitor the difficult, harsh conditions of medical treatment prior to modern times.

Dr. Robert Woodruff Cooke, born in 1797 at Newton, New Jersey, the son of a doctor, began the practice of medicine in 1820 following graduation from the College of Physicians and Surgeons in New York. This two-story, three-room building, erected circa 1823, contains reception and examination rooms on the lower level and a bedroom above. One suspects the latter may have functioned as a recovery room. The Holmdel Historical Society has on extended loan a large variety of Cooke's medical devices and documents. Some among them, such as the circa 1817 amputation set and the glass leech tube (to guide leeches to the appropriate "treatment" site) suggest the primitive state of early medical care and help instill in the visitor a "you are there" feeling for Cooke's times and practice. One of his Physician's Record Books reminds us that local individuals were born and died in his presence. Cooke was also Holmdel's first postmaster, serving from 1830 to 1849.

Cooke continued his medical practice here until his 1897 death. Henry Gansevoort Cooke, Robert's son, was also a physician who maintained his office here until he moved to New Brunswick in 1896. After Henry sold his 120-acre tract in 1909, new owner Theron McCampbell relocated the former medical office that originally stood near the house opposite it now on McCampbell Road. Presumably it was utilized as a farm outbuilding. The office was donated to the Holmdel Historical Society in 1986.

www.holmdelhistory.org; 732.946.2743
Access: by appointment; WOM. Parking: few spaces on site; lot in adjacent Village School.

Holmes-Hendrickson House (NRHP 1978)
62 Longstreet Road
Holmdel, NJ 07733

The expanse of northern Monmouth County that spans Middletown, Holmdel, Colts Neck and Marlboro represents the southern limits of the significant seventeenth-century Dutch settlement that was centered in the Hudson River Valley counties north of New York City. The Holmes-Hendrickson House, one of the finest, architecturally significant, least-changed and well-preserved houses

The two national origins of the house's namesakes are reflected by construction where an English Georgian exterior contains a Dutch-style interior, notably a great room that dominates the floor plan.

to emerge from that period and culture, also represents the Dutch blending into the dominant English social structure of Monmouth County. The house portrays this by combining interior Dutch elements within a Georgian-style house.

Obadiah Holmes, an Englishman and the namesake of Holmdel, bought a sizable area farm in 1716 that passed to his son, Jonathan, who had married a Dutch Hendrickson, and in 1752 to his grandson, William. In 1756, William sold the property to his cousin, Garret Hendrickson, for a sum that was a considerable advance over his purchase price, a transaction that supports the belief that the five-bay main block of the house was built during his short stay. This evidence is also bolstered by the emergence in Monmouth County of the Georgian style in the early 1750s. The Georgian exterior symmetry, which is evidenced through door and window placement, was given prominent Dutch influence through its flared roof and overhanging eaves. The two large front rooms reflect a Dutch living style arrangement, as does the rare enclosed staircase in the rear of the main house. The one-and-a-half-story wing, which predates the main house, may have been the earlier Holmes residence.

The house, which was originally built on a site about a mile to the east, was relocated here circa 1960 preparatory to the construction of Bell Laboratories, which donated it to the Monmouth County Historical Association; the association opened the house to the public in 1963. The moving of a building is typically an impediment to National Register listing, but the age, significance and excellent condition readily enabled this house to overcome that potential barrier at the time of its application. The dark brick-red color was applied in 2008 after paint research determined that this was the house's original hue. The shade, called Spanish Brown in its time, was a popular and economical paint color made from iron oxide. The association sold the property's development rights through a conservation easement to the County of Monmouth in 2011.

www.monmouthhistory.org
Access: 1:00–4:00 p.m. May–September; WOM. Parking: lot.

Horn Antenna
Alcatel-Lucent Bell Labs (NRHP 1989)
791 Keyport-Holmdel Road
Holmdel, NJ 07733

The Bell Laboratories division of the former American Telephone and Telegraph Company attained many firsts and made numerous scientific

The big-bang theory of the universe's creation has entered the general lexicon. This is the instrument on the site where then Bell Telephone Laboratories scientists made their landmark discovery.

discoveries, notably in telecommunications. Their nearby architecturally distinctive and significant Crawfords Corner–Everett Road facility is better known, but a monumental discovery was made at their Crawfords Hill location. One instrument, the Horn Antenna, stands out.

Bell Labs scientists used this antenna in 1965 to detect cosmic background radiation, a discovery that helped confirm the big-bang theory of the creation of the universe. While this twenty-foot horn reflector was built for satellite communications research, its ultimate utility led to a discovery of such merit and value that researchers Arno Penzias and Robert Wilson were awarded the Nobel Prize for physics in 1978.

The Horn Antenna has been occupying a place along with numerous scientific instruments in a field atop a hill above the building's parking lot. The future of the facility, now owned by Alcatel-Lucent, is in question, which may make perilous the well-being of the instruments. The significance of the Horn Antenna is reflected by its 1990 designation as a National Historic Landmark, stature that demands its preservation and prominence.

Access: permission by owner. Parking: open field space around instruments.

Longstreet Farm (NRHP 1979)
44 Longstreet Road
Holmdel, NJ 07733

Longstreet is an active, working, demonstration historic farm, where visitors can see a wide array of agricultural buildings, watch farm operations and enter a historic house.

The farm is named for Hendrik Longstreet, who amassed a 495-acre tract through purchase of smaller farms, including one from his grandfather, Hendrick Hendrickson, who built the large, now rare Dutch barn. This type structure is characterized by long sloping roofs, high wagon doors at the gable end and their most impressive structural members: massive H-shaped anchor bents formed by two end posts connected with a large horizontal anchor beam. They are readily visible inside the barn. Longstreet's, which are twenty-eight-feet long, create a wide central space for threshing, while poles laid across the bents provided hay storage in the loft above. A dozen farm structures are described in a park brochure available at the site.

While the house appears older at first glance than its 1890 date, both Longstreet Farm and the house are interpreted historically for that time in its long history.

The house was built in three sections between 1775 and 1840. Its interior finishing was restored to the late Victorian period of the interpreted agricultural operation, a project that removed twentieth-century modifications.

www.monmouthcountyparks.com; 732.946.3758
Access: farm, daily; farm house, seasonal, weekends and holidays; WOM. Parking: lot.

New Jersey Vietnam Veterans Memorial and Vietnam Era Museum & Educational Center
Garden State Parkway at Exit 116 (1 Memorial Lane)
Holmdel, NJ 07733

The memorial and museum are separate facilities that have a joint mission; they share a common site to honor veterans of the war and educate the public.

The New Jersey Vietnam Veterans Memorial Commission, established by the legislature, was signed into law in 1986. The commission chose to locate its memorial on a five-and-a-half-acre site on the grounds of the Garden State Arts Center. The winner of a design competition was Hien Nguyen,

The Educational Center Building is adjacent to the parking lot, while this circular memorial with polished granite stones is located behind it a short distance to the west. It is the structure prominent to passersby on the northbound lanes of the Garden State Parkway.

a South Vietnam refugee, who planned a two-hundred-foot-diameter open-air circular pavilion fitted with 366 black granite panels on which would be engraved the names of the state's killed or missing. Each panel represents one date of the year. There are over 1,550 names engraved. A nonprofit foundation was created in 1987 to raise the finances and provide managerial assistance for the project's fulfillment. While the groundbreaking ceremony took place on May 7, 1995, a two-and-a-half-year fundraising effort was required before construction began.

The memorial was dedicated on May 7, 1995. The central sculptural assemblage was executed by Thomas Jay Warren. His three figures represent the war's casualties, the women who served and all veterans. Another sculptural memorial, located adjacent to the path from the parking lot to the state's Vietnam memorial, is Bruce Lindsay's United States War Dogs Memorial. The memorial is open twenty-four hours every day to fulfill a mission that "strives to encourage and foster patriotism and provide for recognition of the sacrifices, courage and valor of the New Jersey Veterans of the Vietnam Era."

The Vietnam Era Museum & Educational Center tells the story of the war from both military and homefront perspectives. The building contains exhibition areas, a theater and a multipurpose room that is utilized for educational and related functions. The ten-thousand-square-foot center was dedicated on September 27, 1998.

www.njvvmf.org; 732.335.0033
Access to the memorial: 24 hours, year-round; access to the museum: Tuesday–Saturday, 10:00 a.m.–4:00 p.m. and select patriotic holidays. Parking: lot.

KEYPORT

Keyport Fire Museum
86 Broad Street
Keyport, NJ 07735

Many firefighting organizations are founded and built after a devastating toll from a major blaze. The establishment of the Keyport department was an outgrowth of the 1877 conflagration that destroyed several blocks in town. Keyport not only built a fine fire department, but the department also established the only firefighting museum in the county.

Modern fire apparatus has become so large that one needs to stretch his imagination to realize that this small building did house fire equipment at the turn of the twentieth century.

The museum is located in the former Raritan Hose Company No. 2 firehouse that was built in 1900, moved to this site in 1919 and served until 1969. While the building was occupied as retail space, the museum, assisted by a generous grant, adapted the building for exhibition purposes and opened the museum in October 2003. On display are old apparatus, fire memorabilia of a wide variety and a firefighting research library.

www.keyportfd.org; 732.739.5362
Access: Saturday, 1:00–5:00 p.m.; Sunday, 10:00 a.m.–2:00 p.m., April–December.
Parking: street.

Bayshore Region

Steamboat Dock Museum
2 Broad Street
Keyport, NJ 07735

The early history of shipping from the shore of Raritan Bay embraced a series of small landings located in close proximity where each served a local farming clientele in a transport environment. Multiple docks were required as produce and goods needed to be taken to the shore over poor to nonexistent roads, which was as great a challenge as the subsequent water-borne shipment. Matawan, then reached by a navigable Matawan Creek that could accept oceangoing vessels, was a major shipping point for a long spell, past the midway point of the nineteenth century. Keyport took a major share of the business by providing a dock that could be accessed by the early railroad that reached into the agricultural heartland of Monmouth County. This line became known as the Freehold and New York Railroad when it reached Keyport in 1881, the destination city chosen because a deepwater dock was built in Keyport, which was then able to handle with ease New York traffic. Keyport was also home to a number of shipbuilders and maritime owners and shippers who erected some of the borough's finest residences in the heyday of Bayshore shipping.

The profoundly changed Keyport waterfront has few reminders of its time as a major Monmouth port. This building once served for various maritime functions.

The Steamboat Dock Museum is located on Borough of Keyport property in a former working waterfront building that once contained a ticket office, machine shop and crew quarters. The Keyport Historical Society owns and operates the museum that commemorates, collects and exhibits the history of the town and its maritime past. Special interest is given to the Thomas Kearney Key Grove Plantation, the former estate that is at the core of Keyport's origins and the Aeromarine Plane and Motor Corporation, a local manufacturer that was a major force in the early years of aviation. Changing exhibits, along with a vast array of artifacts and print material, fill the museum.

www.keyportonline.com; 732.739.6390
Access: Sundays, mid-May–end of September; events; WOM. Parking: adjacent lot.

MATAWAN

Burrowes Mansion Museum (NRHP 1972)
94 Main Street
Matawan, NJ 07747

The Burrowes Mansion is one of Monmouth County's most important early Georgian buildings, although its history is clouded by legend and an incomplete documentary trail. It was the site of a clash during the Revolution and was noteworthy throughout the development of the future borough of Matawan.

Stylistic evidence dates the original house as circa 1750 when the Georgian style was introduced to Monmouth County. The two-and-a-half-story main block was a Georgian three-bay side-hall plan. Historical inference suggests that John Burrowes Sr. (1718–1785) may have acquired the property around the time of his 1749 marriage to widow Hope Taylor Watson (1721–1792). Perhaps the earlier date attributed to the house stems from the sale of the property in 1722, but this house could not be as early as the circa 1723 date recorded in the Historic American Buildings Survey, the National Register nomination or the historical plaque outside the house. Burrowes was a major grain and produce merchant who earned the nickname "Corn King." His property backed on Matawan Creek, once a major waterway that handled oceangoing sailing ships, when the town, part of Middletown Township until 1848, was known as Middletown Point to reflect stature as the Bayshore's major port.

A major appeal of Matawan's Main Streetscape is a fine collection of houses that range in time for over a century and a half. The Burrowes Mansion claims the greatest historic stature.

In 1778 during the Revolution, Loyalists attempted to capture Burrowes's son, also John, a Continental army captain who was a co-organizer of troops composing the First New Jersey Company. He escaped, but his wife was injured, and the father was captured, although he was soon released in a prisoner exchange. The Loyalists reportedly burned his mills, granaries, storehouses and furniture.

The property was designated for John Jr. in his father's will, but documentary history over the next four decades is vague until the house and fifteen acres were sold to Joseph H. and Holmes Van Mater in 1825. Later the Burrowes Mansion was a hotel, a dentist's residence (and presumably office), a tea room and under the ownership and occupancy of Benjamin F.S. Brown, whose family retained the place until its 1974 sale to the Borough of Matawan. The Matawan Historical Society, founded in 1969, furnishes and operates the restored house, one that retains a strong character of its colonial roots.

www.matawanborough.com; 732.566.5605
Access: first and third Sundays March–December; events; WOM. Parking: street and small lot in rear.

MIDDLETOWN

All Saints Memorial Church (Protestant Episcopal) (NRHP 1974)
202 Navesink Avenue (PO Box 326)
Navesink, NJ 07752

This fine English Gothic church designed by Richard Upjohn is significant for its architectural stature, its early date that preceded the major urban summer migration to the area and its physical layout, one readily apparent even to the casual viewer, a hilltop setting with a collection of related church structures.

The Milnor and Stephens families, Newark residents who founded All Saints as a private chapel, employed Upjohn, the noted architect who is famed for Trinity Church in New York among his numerous Gothic Revival masterpieces. Following the laying of the cornerstone on October 7, 1863, the congregation organized formally the next year when the church was consecrated as a memorial to deceased members of their families. The parish house followed in 1866, while the rectory was completed in 1870. All were built of an appealing local peanut stone, a material also utilized in the adjoining cemetery. The interior, more intimate than the church's

Note the church's construction of local peanut stone. This material was also used in its rectory, parish house and the cemetery, all set on an unchanged lot that readily lets ones imagination step back into the late nineteenth century.

imposing siting on the hill may suggest, is richly decorated with memorial stained-glass windows.

The restored carriage sheds from the turn of the twentieth century are a reminder that early worshippers traveled by horse. The cemetery merits an inspection, notably for artistic stone of its early period. While there, look for the prominent sculpted bust of actor Neil Burgess. The small congregation, which relates to its area as a community-oriented asset, welcomes visitors with a variety of programs that include music. All Saints was designated a National Historic Landmark in 1988. The church's location is nearly adjacent to the Navesink Historic District and on a prominent back road to Twin Lights. If taking the Monmouth Avenue route, one can access the Mount Mitchill Scenic Overlook by crossing Highway 36 and following the signs to the parking area. This site includes the Monmouth County September 11 Memorial and offers a fine view of the nearby harbor and New York in the distance.

www.allsaintsnavesink.org; 732.291.0214
Access: worship; events; WOM. Parking: lot.

Brookdale Farm
Brookdale Community College
765 Newman Springs Road
Lincroft, NJ 07738

Monmouth County Park System Headquarters
805 Newman Springs Road
Lincroft, NJ 07738

Monmouth Museum
765 Newman Springs Road
Lincroft, NJ 07738

Brookdale was a major horse stock farm in the latter decades of the nineteenth and early decades of the twentieth centuries. Reminiscences of

Major Brookdale Farm buildings were incorporated into the design of Brookdale Community College, but also this original corncrib that now provides protected seating in the midst of a walkway.

The rebuilt Thompson Park Visitors Center is virtually indistinguishable from the earliest photograph of the house, which was constructed by William P. Thompson.

The stone of the Monmouth Museum is reminiscent of the nearby school structures. The varied exhibition program has an artistic bent.

that famed establishment are spread throughout its environs that have been given to adaptive use for parks and education.

In 1872, David D. Withers, a nationally known horseman and an organizer of Monmouth Park, began amassing Lincroft parcels that would reach eight hundred acres. He founded and named Brookdale Farm and kept a summer residence near its western edge at the site of today's park Visitors Center. Withers is remembered by his namesake stakes race that is still run in Aqueduct Park, New York.

After William P. Thompson, another significant horseman, bought Brookdale in 1893, he hired Carrere and Hastings to envelop the Withers house with the fine Classical Revival structure like today's Visitors Center. Following William's death in 1896, his son, Lewis Steenrod Thompson, presided over Brookdale, but since he lacked his father's equine interests, Brookdale was leased over the next few decades, often to the famed Whitney racing stable. Lewis's widow, the former Geraldine Livingston Morgan, remained after his 1936 death to become the best-known figure at Brookdale as a consequence of her public benefactions, political prominence and long stay until her passing in 1967. She bequeathed 215 acres to establish the Monmouth County Thompson Park, while another 220 acres were sold for the county's Brookdale Community College.

Today the recreational and educational usage of Brookdale Farm is fulfilled in a historical environment that has retained much of the character of the former horse farm. Planners have accomplished this by the retention of many historic structures and the skillful adaptive use of others. The famed Thompson mansion, which became the Visitors Center, was destroyed by fire on February 5, 2006, but a faithful reconstruction retains its image and made only relatively minor interior changes necessary to accommodate current building codes and functionality. Visitors should take special note of the retained farm structures, including a massive barn, west of the center.

Most of the early college buildings were adaptive uses by Red Bank architect Bernard Kellenyi. New buildings from the school's major expansion over the last quarter of the twentieth century typically blend well with the older built environment.

The home of the Monmouth Museum was built on the Brookdale campus in 1974 after the organization utilized temporary storefront locations, usually in Red Bank, following its 1963 founding as a "museum of ideas." An imaginative, flexible approach to exhibitions and diverse spheres of interest have brought forth over the years displays on a variety of artistic, natural, historical and scientific subjects. In the recent past, exhibitions in their principal spaces have focused on a variety of artistic subjects. Two special areas for children have been effective to introducing younger visitors to the museum experience, typically by utilizing scientific subjects that engage them.

College: www.brookdalecc.edu; 732.224.2345
Park system: www.monmouthcountyparks.com; 732.842.4000
Museum: www.monmouthmuseum.org; 732.747.2266
Parking for all sites: lots.

Christ Church (NRHP 1971)
90 Kings Highway
Middletown, NJ 07748

The Middletown Christ Church dates its origins from the Christmas 1702 communion worship at Lewis Morris's Tinton Falls home, as does its Shrewsbury counterpart. The two were at one time a joint congregation that was chartered by King George II in 1738.

A church was built on this corner in the eighteenth century, located on the site of a former blockhouse, a type of fortification. This edifice was constructed in 1835 on the foundation of the earlier building. The two churches split into separate parishes in 1854 after dividing common property.

This Christ Church edifice was built in 1835 atop an earlier foundation, prior to the separation in 1854 of this church from Christ Church, Shrewsbury, with which it was once a joint parish.

Adjacent on the west are the Leeds Hall parish house built in 1950 and a 1965 building that combines modern worship space and educational space.

www.christchurchmiddletown.org; 732.671.2524
Access:worship; Parking: street.

Fair View Cemetery
456 Highway 35
Red Bank NJ 07701
(mailing and GPS address for a Middletown location)

Private and church burying grounds—look for those in the Middletown Village historic district—were the norm until about the second quarter of the nineteenth century. Not only was space a concern, but it was also realized that larger, well-designed cemeteries could provide an ancillary benefit of respite at a time when both leisure and available public areas were scarce.

The older sections of Fair View Cemetery are particularly artistic and reminiscent of the time when early cemeteries were planned for their leisure and recreational potential.

The movement for cemeteries as beautiful parks became apparent in eastern Monmouth County by the middle of the nineteenth century. This need culminated in the opening of Fair View in 1855 when leading local citizens established a nonprofit organization that built the early sections, beautiful parklike grounds laid out by Ezra A. Osborn. Fair View's two entrances are on the south side of Highway 35 and the west side of Oak Hill Road.

Fair View includes a variety of monuments that exhibit changing funerary practice. Some graves predate the cemetery's 1855 founding, reinterments made after a variety of circumstances threatened older private burying grounds. While historians tend to focus on the cemetery's northern end, where stones read as a who's who of regional history, the newer sections near the railroad exhibit a marked change in memorial custom. Its acreage, originally 47, has expanded to 175. Much of it remains undeveloped, which will allow for expansion into the distant future.

An important eye-catching public monument stands inside the Highway 35 entrance, a memorial to the Twenty-ninth Regiment of New Jersey Volunteer Infantry. Its late dedication date of May 30, 1925, makes it likely that it is the last of the significant New Jersey Civil War monuments installed during the lifetime of its veterans. The Chaplain Hill monument, an earlier stone with a Civil War tie, was dedicated on October 14, 1909, to honor the Reverend Charles E. Hill, who served twenty years as chaplain of the local chapter of the Grand Army of the Republic. A monument honoring all veterans was dedicated May 20, 1995, in conjunction with Fair View's opening of a veterans' section.

Nearby, Mount Olivet Cemetery is a short distance to the north on Chapel Hill Road. Here one can compare Catholic funerary practices with the nonsectarian Fair View. Mount Olivet claims two noteworthy monuments, the grave of legendary football coach Vince Lombardi and the twenty-six-foot-high monument to local priests.

732.747.1710
Access: grounds open from sunrise to sunset. Parking: along paths where space permits.

Fort Hancock and Proving Ground Historic District (NRHP 1982)
(Gateway National Recreation Area, Sandy Hook)
84 Mercer Road
Middletown Township, NJ 07732

Fort Hancock's career as a significant coastal defensive facility began at the time of the Spanish-American War and endured into the Cold War. It was arguably the most heavily fortified shore fort during most of that time. A companion army presence, its proving grounds for decades tested all of the heavy weaponry that was issued to our fighting forces. Many of their built environments stand, although in pitifully neglected condition.

The value of Sandy Hook as a defensive fortification to protect the surrounding area from naval incursion was apparent at the time of the purchase of the land in 1814 from the Hartshorne family. Indeed, its strategic importance was demonstrated during the Revolution, during which Sandy Hook was held by British and Loyalist forces. Although progress to plan and build a defensive fortification was slow, the significant effort begun by 1859 was halted by the Civil War and then abandoned as advances in offensive weapons made during the war rendered the fort as planned obsolete. Postwar efforts lagged, notably due to the reluctance of Congress to allocate

The disappearing carriage gun demonstrates one old development in the contest of offensive and defensive weaponry at Fort Hancock. This gun, in ready-to-fire position (after the crew gets off), would be lifted over the wall by counterweights, then returned after discharging its projectile to be concealed behind that barrier. *Courtesy of Michael Steinhorn.*

funds; during this period the country became increasingly vulnerable to naval bombardment. The planning of the 1880s resulted in the 1890 start of construction for a fort that was named in 1895 for Civil War general Winfield Scott Hancock and turned over to the operational control of the coast artillery department on March 22, 1898.

Armaments and the practices to protect these arms changed regularly at the fort, as the developers of offensive weapons and defensive protection regularly "dueled" to attain superiority. Many of the gun emplacements, usually called batteries, are intact but often in precarious condition; some are closed to visitors. Park brochures describe their operation. The last weapon employed was the NIKE antiaircraft missile during the Cold War. Some, as has been revealed only in recent years, were armed with nuclear warheads. NIKEs were operational until 1974 when the deployment of Soviet intercontinental ballistic missiles made antiaircraft weapons obsolete.

Buildings once utilized for a variety of functions are located throughout the fort. They are typically made of yellow brick and were used for barracks, residential, storage and other purposes. Many are in deteriorated and unusable condition. They, too, are identified and explained by park interpretive material. The large open space in the midst of the fort buildings was a parade grounds.

The proving grounds were not only separate from the fort, but the grounds' 1874 establishment actually preceded the formal establishment of the fort. The proving operation tested weapons that were intended for active forces to ensure that poorly made guns did not explode or suffer other accident when placed into service. Some tested guns did explode, and at times with loss of life. The proving grounds buildings are typically red brick. A concrete platform that made up Proof Battery, that now contains interpretive material, is located near the North Beach parking lot. This information will help the visitor understand how weapons were tested. Their firing down the long narrow expanse of beach of Sandy Hook in close proximity to a railroad made the practice potentially dangerous, and in 1919, the proving operation was relocated to Aberdeen, Maryland. The proving grounds also tested defensive armament by, for example, firing shells of a certain charge into steel plates that replicated armor.

A number of other organizations occupy Sandy Hook in or near the fort, some in newer buildings, others adaptively using former fort buildings. These tenants may increase in coming years, as the federal government is eager to obtain compatible occupancies by tenants who will undertake restoration of buildings they would occupy.

Specific places to see (check for open hours) include a museum, the post theater, chapel, the officers' row residential building occupied as History House and, south of the fort area, the visitors center which is the former Life Saving Station No. 1. This structure was built in 1891 to replace the original building that was erected in 1849 at the dawn of this federal operation to rescue seafarers along a dangerous stretch of eastern coast. The Coast Guard station at the northern tip of the Hook is not accessible by the public.

Nearby, during World War II, the army installed a battery with sixteen-inch guns in what is now Hartshorne Woods Park, which is owned and operated by the County of Monmouth. The dock of Naval Weapons Station Earle, nearby to the west, which opened in 1944, is clearly visible from many local perspectives. This pier was the principal shipping point for naval weapons used in the European theater during World War II.

www.nps.gov/gate and www.sandyhookfoundation.org; 732.872.5970.
Access: park and beach, daily, sunrise to sunset; visitors center, 10:00 a.m.–5:00 p.m. daily. Parking: designated areas; do not use beach parking in season to avoid parking fee.

Sandy Hook Lighthouse (Gateway National Recreation Area)
84 Mercer Road
Middletown Township, NJ 07732

The Sandy Hook Lighthouse is one of the most significant in America and is the county's oldest operating lighthouse. It was erected by New York shipping and merchant interests in order to increase navigational safety at the narrow channel at the entrance to the city's harbor. It is now the historical highlight of the Sandy Hook Unit of Gateway National Recreation Area.

The lighthouse was financed by lottery authorized by the New York legislature and built on land purchased from the Hartshorne family; the light

This close-up image emphasizes how much wider the base is than the top of the lighthouse, a consequence of the walls bearing the weight of the structure.

on the 103-foot tower was first lit on June 11, 1764. The beacon was then located about 500 feet from the tip of the Sandy Hook barrier beach, but accretions from the force of tides and the erosion of cliffs farther south along the shore have extended the length of the Hook, placing the light about one and a half miles from the tip now.

The lighthouse's strategic importance during the Revolution occasioned an attempt by rebel forces to destroy it by artillery fire on June 21, 1776. The Loyalists retained occupancy throughout the war, while the British used the area following their withdrawal from the Battle of Monmouth to depart for their New York destination. The light passed to federal government ownership in 1790. The light was maintained by a keeper who initially lived in a house adjacent to the light, but in 1883, his residence was relocated to the extant house nearby. He at one point had charge of three lights, a lesser beacon on the north, necessitated by the lengthening distance of the main light from the tip, and another on the west bordering the river where the light helped mark a bay channel. The north beacon was removed in 1917 for relocation on the Hudson River where it is now under the New York tower of the George Washington Bridge. The west beacon was removed at an unknown year in the latter 1930s.

A third-order Fresnel lens was installed in 1857, the year the lens house was added to the tower. The lighthouse has used a variety of illuminants over the years, notably a variety of oils. The first unsuccessful attempt to electrify was made in 1896, but permanent electrification was not installed until the 1920s. A major renovation was made in 1863 when a red brick lining to reinforce the walls was built and the iron spiral staircase installed.

The octagonal Sandy Hook lighthouse, instantly recognizable by its tapered appearance, narrows from a twenty-nine-foot base to fifteen feet at the top of the wall. Deeply etched in maritime culture, the lighthouse has appeared on two postage stamps. It was designated a National Historic Landmark in 1964 and rededicated on June 11, 1976. While its Fresnel lens is still present, the continuously lit light is primarily decorative now. It is visible about 19.0 miles at sea under ideal weather conditions, but the light as maritime aid was transferred in 1967 to a now unmanned light platform located 7.4 miles off shore. On the National Parks Service's website, there is a description of the park, while elsewhere can be found a lighthouse brochure. A web search will find the lighthouse mentioned, often in detail, on many other sites.

www.nps.gov/gate; 7328725970
Access: park, daily; lighthouse tours, summer weekends; WOM. Parking: lot

MacLeod-Rice House
900 Leonardville Road
Leonardo, (Middletown Township) NJ
(Mail: PO Box 180, Middletown, NJ 07748)

The storied past of the MacLeod-Rice House embraces marital intrigue, the advance of sanitary dairy farming, presidential politics and educational history. It is owned by the Township of Middletown as the centerpiece of its park system headquarters on the Croydon Hall campus.

The story began when the fifty-two-year-old Donald W. MacLeod married twenty-five-year-old Harriet Bush in 1889. They resided in Brooklyn, near his New York business interest of the import of Belgian linens. In 1894, he bought land on the emerging country house settlement of Highland Park. It was under development on the former Edward Burdge farm where MacLeod bought his house lot and built in front of the former Burdge residence a Queen Anne–style mansion designed by L. Jerome Aimar of Atlantic Highlands that was intended for summer occupancy. After becoming ill later in the decade, MacLeod was kept in isolation at his Brooklyn residence,

Donald MacLeod's original Queen Anne–style house was obliterated by Melvin Rice's Classical Revival remodeling done around 1910, giving the place its present image. The image is dated 1986.

where he was not permitted visitors, even his family, who accused his wife of denying him treatment. It was apparent that Harriet was having an affair with Melvin A. Rice, a minor Brooklyn Democratic political figure, whose wife was then planning to divorce him. After MacLeod died in 1901, Rice, who was reticent about his relationship with the widow, married her in secret the next year. After also succeeding MacLeod to the business and the Middletown house, one could say that Rice made his money the old-fashioned way: he married it.

Rice remodeled the place circa 1910, using another Atlantic Highlands architect, Thomas Emery, to give the house its present Classical Revival appearance. Rice also added the library wing on the east, in part to display his hunting trophies. He was also active with agricultural operations, including a model dairy farm, built at a time when gentlemen farmers were in the forefront of emerging sanitary milk operations. After Rice befriended then governor Woodrow Wilson, he offered his house as a refuge from the crowds that descended on the governor's Sea Girt summer home following Wilson's 1912 presidential nomination. Not only was Wilson a regular visitor here, but after his ascension to the presidency, it was thought that Rice might be serving as his emissary during his business travel to Europe in the early years of World War I, prior to the American involvement. Rice became a benefactor of local education and was chosen president of the New Jersey Board of Education. After his December 31, 1924 death, his widow stayed, but her finances were devastated. The property came into the possession of John M. Carr, a Boston educator, who opened his Croydon Hall Academy in 1947, a private boy's boarding school. While the school enjoyed stature in its early years as the only area boarding school, it struggled as local educational opportunities improved. Croydon Hall later became coeducational, but after years of coping with enrollment and financial problems, the school succumbed after the 1975–76 academic year. The Bayshore Christian School opened in its place, but it failed after one year. Subsequently, the Township of Middletown acquired the property for park purposes. As Croydon Hall Academy had built up its campus over the years, the township was able to acquire substantial brick offices in former classrooms, a gym and other modern space. The Middletown Township Historical Society has occupied the grade floor of the maintenance-challenged former house since 1984. The surrounding athletic facilities have expanded over the years.

In the region, the adjacent Beacon Hill Country Club includes along its fairways a few houses that were also part of the Highland Park development. Another contemporary, more successful colony of summer houses was built in the township a few miles to the east above Highway 36. The former Water Witch Park is a National Register historic district, now known as Monmouth Hills. It consists of a fine collection of primarily Shingle– and other period style houses on grounds that can be driven by entering at the traffic circle on the highway's eastbound lane at Linden Avenue.

Access: events including meetings of the Middletown Township Historical Society. Parking: lot in rear.

Marlpit Hall (Monmouth County Historical Association)
137 Kings Highway
Middletown, NJ 07748

Marlpit Hall is the circa 1756 homestead of the Taylors, a family that is one of Monmouth County's most significant early settlers that were extensive property owners in Middletown Township. The house was the home of Edward Taylor, whose actions in conjunction with his son George's Loyalist

Marlpit Hall is distinguished as the region's first restored house museum. The entire building was determined through structural analysis to date from the mid-eighteenth century. This recent research dispelled an earlier belief of a major addition made at that time to a late seventeenth-century structure.

military activity during the American Revolution led to his house arrest and the loss of much family wealth and local respect. The subsequent rising fortunes of the Taylors are reflected in their ability to build the adjoining residence, listed as the Taylor-Butler House but historically known as the Orchard Home. When it was erected circa 1853, Orchard Home was the finest and grandest in the region. Marlpit Hall, a name coined when the house entered association ownership, is also significant for its opening as Monmouth County's first restored house museum.

An extensive historic structures report in the late 1990s revealed the true origins of a house with a long written history. The study indicated evidence of an earlier house, probably late seventeenth-century, which was apparently taken down when the present house was begun around 1756. The report revealed that construction in that time was accomplished by two carpenters serving two successive owners that resulted in a house with significant interior differences, which perhaps contributed to the former "two house" belief. Ownership passed through a number of Taylors, beginning with the aforementioned Edward's son, John, then John's son, Edward, and subsequently his daughter, Mary Holmes Taylor. Taylor family history continues in the following entry and their construction of the Taylor-Butler House.

The old house and future Marlpit Hall became affectionately known as the "Grandfather Farm" and was leased to tenant farmers, a period in which its condition deteriorated. Destruction was threatened in 1911 by a realignment of Kings Highway, but the family insisted that the house be preserved through moving it to its present location. Following the 1930 death of the second Mary Holmes Taylor, the last Taylor to own the property, Marlpit Hall was bought by Margaret Riker Haskell (Mrs. J. Amory) in 1935, one of the nation's foremost collectors of Americana, notably fine antique furniture. She undertook repairs, furnished the house and gave Marlpit Hall to the association the next year. The house, which has undergone interpretive changes over the decades, retains stature as the region's first house museum and the western anchor of the Middletown Village historic district.

www.monmouthhistory.org; 732.462.1466
Access: 1:00–4:00 p.m. Thursday–Saturday, May–September; WOM. Parking: lot in rear and lot at adjacent Village School.

Taylor-Butler House (Monmouth County Historical Association)
127 Kings Highway
Middletown, NJ 07748

The Taylor-Butler House embraces the story of the rise and fall of the family fortune of the Taylors. When the Italianate mansion was built by Joseph Dorset Taylor around 1853, it was the largest and grandest residence in the region. When his daughter died there in 1930, the house lacked indoor plumbing. Without compromise to the house's integrity, it has been brought into the modern era but instantly conveys its mid-nineteenth-century elegance to both casual visitor and those who may wish to plan an event here.

Continuing the family background from the Marlpit entry above, Loyalist Edward's great-granddaughter, Mary Holmes Taylor, who had assumed ownership of the Middletown property, married her first cousin, Joseph Dorset Taylor, in 1846 at a time when romantic opportunities were likely few. He was a prosperous merchant in the China trade. They built this house upon retirement from New York to Middletown, had a son, another Edward, and daughter, also Mary Holmes Taylor. The traditional

The Taylor-Butler House was the largest and grandest of its era, but it is little changed from this 1886 image.

name Orchard Home stemmed from its siting amid the Marlpit Hall orchards. After the elder Taylor died in 1864, the daughter, who never married, cared for her mother until the latter's death in 1897. While the son had no known occupation, he was a serious photographer who left a valuable oeuvre that vividly depicted his house and surrounding area in the 1890–1910 era.

The Taylor children apparently lived off a dwindling family fortune. While they once employed household servants, during the younger Mary's final decade, the 1920s, her house lacked indoor plumbing. Her estate that was dispersed after her 1930 death included numerous family heirlooms. The house was bought in 1941 by architect Henry Ludwig Kramer, who repaired and made the place fit for modern use. George and Helen Butler, who were socially active in the village community, became the third and final private owners in 1954. Following George's death in 1998, the association acquired the house the next year under favorable terms, which prompted its renaming that honors the Butler family. Thus, the association, deeply rooted in the colonial era through its four other properties (all described herein), was thrust into the nineteenth century. Their acquisition, however, naturally fit with adjoining Marlpit Hall since it permits a two-century interpretation of a foremost Monmouth family. While the other association houses are furnished, Taylor-Butler is not, but it is used for association functions and is available for rental from them for private events.

www.monmouthhistory.org; 732.462.1466
Access: events; WOM. The house is available for rental for certain functions. Park: small lot in rear and in Village School adjacent to Marlpit Hall.

Middletown Village Historic District (NRHP 1974)
Along Kings Highway
Middletown, NJ 07748

The district's significance stems from both its number of major well-preserved buildings and a layout that embraces its 1667 nucleated town center design, a concept brought from New England that clustered residents and their public buildings in close proximity. Early settlers also owned extensive farms, or "outlots," which were located throughout the region. Three major public buildings in this district are listed separately: Marlpit Hall (page 42), Christ

Church (page 32) and Old First Church (page 49). Much of the district consists of private residences that can be readily viewed from the street. When observing them, please be respectful of the owners' privacy.

As one travels in an easterly direction from the district's western boundary at Marlpit Hall, one finds the Dutch Reformed Church at 121 Kings Highway. The church was built in 1836, but the exterior reflects the alterations of 1898–99. The church's establishment denotes the early influence of Dutch settlers in northern Monmouth County, an area that represented the southernmost reach of the Dutch settlement that was centered in the Hudson River Valley. A second notable public building is a block to the east, the former blacksmith shop on the southwest corner of Conover Avenue. The first of the significant houses is the Greek Revival residence at 109. The origins of the Dr. Taylor house at number 82 date circa 1725, but the place's expansions were later. Number 78, which was built around 1930 as a telephone exchange and attendant's home, was later the township's library but has been converted to a residence. These two houses are separated by the block-long Hartshorne Place. The Middletown September 11 Memorial is located a block to the south at its end. The portraits and quotations engraved on the stones of the memorial honoring the township's thirty-seven victims of the terrorist attack make this among the most moving of the nation's many memorials.

Number 65, long known as Richard Hartshorne's retirement home, was built by a Hendrickson in the first quarter of the eighteenth century. The Gothic Revival number 61 was built as the Baptist parsonage, while number 53 was completed in 1837 as the Franklin Academy, initially a private school, then part of the public system, later a library and finally remodeled as a residence. The "Pink House," a nickname not quite the color of the terracotta block fabric of number 46 is fascinating for its construction material. Note the Presbyterian Cemetery at the southwest corner of Kings Place. A church of affiliation with this burying ground has not been located. A fine Colonial Revival stands at number 49, one that blends well with its older neighbors. Number 35 is an eighteenth-century survivor but only the rear part, as the impressive main block was built in two sections in the nineteenth century. The other properties consist of houses of varying age that either contribute to the district through age or artistry or are modern additions that do not represent historical interest. The historical plaques note the route of the British marching through the area after the Battle of Monmouth.

Access: public streets. Parking: along street; on the weekends, nearby Middletown railroad lot.

Joseph Murray Farm House at Poricy Park
345 Oak Hill Road (PO Box 30)
Middletown, NJ 07748

An old historically significant house with a critical tie to Middletown's role in the Revolution was uncovered during a project that began as a land preservation campaign by environmentalists concerned over plans for an inappropriate sewer project. The Poricy Park Conservancy operates the Joseph Murray Farm House facility for the Township of Middletown owner, a property that is celebrated and occupied as both a nature center and a historic site.

Multiple Murrays in the historical records led to confusion or simply misapprehension as to where the slain Patriot lived and died. The lack of awareness is likely attributable to a well-known historian who placed Joseph's house on a Kings Highway tract that was owned by another Murray. Perhaps the confusion was reinforced by this tract's locale close to Joseph's monument

Modern additions once obscured the colonial origins of the Joseph Murray farmhouse, which were revealed during restoration. A mid-nineteenth-century section was added to the original.

in the Old First Church Cemetery. Joseph had earned the respect of his compatriots and the enmity of his foes for his rugged adherence to the Patriot cause. He was slain while working his fields in 1782. His death, which could be characterized as a murder, symbolizes the civil war nature of the conflict in Monmouth, a county where neighbor fought neighbor, and a place where hostilities continued for about two years after the surrender at Yorktown. Murray, a stonemason by trade who emigrated from Ireland in 1767, built the origins of this house around 1770. Expanded later, the house remained in the family until 1861. The house continued as a working farm into modern times but fell into a period of decline, as later changes covered its historic origins. After an extensive tract was purchased by the Township of Middletown in 1973, the house was "rediscovered," restored and opened for historical display in conjunction with a nature center operated by the Poricy Park Conservancy.

www.poricypark.org; 732.842.5966
Access: farmhouse, usually last Sunday of month; nature center, usually Sunday–Friday; events; WOM. Parking: lot at Nature Center; Circle adjacent to farmhouse.

Navesink Historic District
Monmouth, Navesink and Hillside Avenues
Middletown, NJ

The Navesink neighborhood represents a largely intact commercial and residential district that in the third quarter of the nineteenth-century—a period that saw the area's greatest growth—was the largest population center in its surrounding rural area.

A number of stores, both grist- and sawmills, hotels, a blacksmith shop, a wheelwright shop and a post office once dotted the district that runs primarily along Monmouth Avenue from near Browns Dock Road to the east side of Lakeside Avenue, with additional pieces along Sears and Navesink Avenues. A small post office remained on the latter, adjoining the surviving store until the late twentieth century. The Navesink United Methodist Church on Navesink Avenue is the oldest congregation in the area, their 1889 edifice standing on the foundation of a simple 1853 predecessor. A Greek Revival building at 175½ Monmouth Avenue, which has 1832 origins as a Baptist house of worship, was later the township's first library before being adapted for residential use. While All Saints (page 28) is a short distance east of the district, its founding and the settlement nearby of its sponsor Milnor and

Stephens families contribute to the area's significance prior to the post–Civil War influx of city summer dwellers. The first of Middletown's volunteer fire companies, which now occupies its third house on the north side of Monmouth Avenue, was founded here in 1886 in a no-longer-extant building on the south side. Much of the Navesink district's charm comes from its compatible mix of houses that span about seven decades of the nineteenth and early twentieth centuries. Later construction blends with the old, creating a pleasant, cohesive whole. Noteworthy from the twentieth century is the Colonial Revival Navesink Library at Monmouth and Sears Avenues.

Access: public streets. Parking: streets.

Old First Church
69 Kings Highway
Middletown, NJ 07748

The Baptist Church in New Jersey was founded here in 1688 at a site historically known as the First Baptist Church. The early flourishing of the faith saw the establishment in the colonial era of many other congregations that point back to Middletown as their mother church.

The Baptist Church in New Jersey was founded on this site in 1688. This is their third edifice, a Greek Revival structure built in 1832.

The standing Greek Revival edifice, the church's third, was built in 1832 on a 1720 foundation. The steeple is a replacement of a taller, narrow one that was destroyed in a May 1890 storm. The Reverend Abel Morgan, who is regarded as one of the most important of the early Baptist clergy who served as a minister for fifty-one years, the last forty-seven at Middletown, is buried in the adjacent cemetery. His prominent monument is a replacement of the original that was destroyed by the falling steeple. Slain Patriot Joseph Murray, whose house is depicted herein, (page 47) is also buried there. Later changes, including 1915 windows in the sanctuary, are best viewed in the appealing interior.

This church was an active participant in a number of nineteenth-century public causes, including social reform, opposition to slavery and temperance. The latter is reflected by the connection on its west of the former Women's Christian Temperance Union building, which was relocated here from nearby Church Street around 1894. Middletown Baptist changed its name to Old First Church following its joint affiliation in 1963 with the United Church of Christ denomination.

www.oldfirstchurchnj.org; 732.671.1905
Access: worship; events; WOM. Parking: lot west of church; angled parking front of church.

Little Red Schoolhouse (NRHP 1976)
Middletown-Lincroft Road at the Southwest Corner of Dwight Road
Middletown, NJ 07748

Educational instruction in the Nut Swamp area—once a significant Middletown neighborhood—began in a nearby private residence and became formalized when moved to this one-room school in 1842; it was an era when numerous similar structures were built in the township and throughout the county. Classroom use continued at what is historically known as Union Schoolhouse No. 9 until about 1907, when new brick schools were built in Lincroft and Middletown village, the start of consolidation. A one-room school at Everett was also closed. Conditions here were primitive, heat was provided by a wood-burning stove, while the restroom was an outhouse that was similar to the later replacement that stands rear of the school.

The Little Red Schoolhouse, while given minor additions since its 1842 origins, bears the unmistakable characteristics of the one-room school. Also note the small structure in the rear, a surviving "necessary," or outhouse, to use the more vivid, if less delicate, term.

The abandoned school, which became part of the Joseph T. Field farm, was utilized for storage, an adaptive use that facilitated its survival. Major John and Mrs. Zanff became the owners in 1937. She was a noteworthy figure in the fashion world, known there as Hattie Carnegie, a name now remembered by two streets adjacent to the school. Following her death in 1961, the estate was sold for development, but the building and its plot were given to the Township of Middletown for public use. Custodianship and use of the building were given to the Garden Club RFD, which has occupied the property since 1954. The building might have maintained a lower profile, but students of the adjacent Thompson Middle School undertook a successful bicentennial-inspired history project to seek listing on the National Register of Historic Places. While infrequently open, the building's prominent corner site suggests how it once contributed to a now forgotten neighborhood that has been absorbed by its surroundings, notably Oak Hill.

Access: infrequent events, e.g. plant sales. Parking: along street where space permits.

Seabrook-Wilson House (NRHP 1974)
719 Port Monmouth Road
Port Monmouth, Middletown Township, NJ 07758

The Seabrook-Wilson House is one of the region's oldest, but it possesses a varied history that is symbolic of the Bayshore and has a preservation survivorship story with recent success elevating the place's public service.

The surrounding land, one of New Jersey's oldest recorded tracts, which dates from the 1660s, belonged to Thomas Whitlock, an owner who never lived here. The house was begun by either Daniel or James Seabrook, who erected the section on the west around the early 1700s on their large farm—or plantation, to use the parlance of the times. The Seabrooks cultivated the land for five generations, while the house was enlarged by a number of expansions, parts added on the east and overhead, as one-story sections were elevated to two full stories. The Reverend William V. Wilson became the most prominent owner after he married two Seabrook sisters (in succession, not concurrently) and oversaw the last of the expansions.

Arguably the oldest surviving house on the Bayshore, the Seabrook-Wilson House suffered both an earlier incarnation as a tavern and ineffective restoration attempts when owned by the Township of Middletown. This contemporary image reflects an authentic and costly restoration undertaken by the County of Monmouth.

He was present for much change, including the section's renaming from Shoal Harbor to Port Monmouth, the arrival of the railroad in 1860 along with a steamship dock to bring train passengers from New York and the development of industry, notably the consolidation of small fish processing operations.

The house was occupied as a tavern for decades in the twentieth century, along with a less decorous use for the many second-floor bedrooms. It became rundown and vacant in the 1960s and was threatened with destruction prior to its purchase in 1967 by the Township of Middletown, which, along with a newly created historical society, undertook preservation measures; many proved inappropriate.

The group fabricated the name "spy house" to "elevate" the place's history and established a museum, alternately called the Spy House or the Shoal Harbor Marine Museum. The "Spy House" took on a life of its own. Revolutionary re-enactors and the postal service were drawn in and the public hoodwinked to believe this was a Revolutionary War site, a myth that is proving exceptionally hard to quell. The place became the Bayshore's "attic," filled with stuff that a generation of schoolchildren passed through and loved. The place made up in popularity what it lacked in authenticity. It endured for decades under the stewardship of curator Gertrude Neidlinger, who, although responsible for saving the place, let her fundraising devolve into a series of controversial ghost tours, which, combined with a lack of fiscal accountability, led to her forced departure in 1993. In 1998, the by-then-vacant building was transferred in a land swap by the township to the County of Monmouth, which undertook a preservation plan.

The county's costly, authentic rehabilitation, including restoration where possible, renewed the vitality of the house and provided the care to assure its long-term viability. The county had earlier established the Bayshore Waterfront Park in the environs; the house has become the headquarters and activity center of the park. This book's publication will be about concurrent with the completion of historical exhibits that will tell the story of the house and its surroundings. The house sits over a small beach on the Raritan Bay. Not to be missed is the superlative view with the New York skyline readily visible on a clear day.

www.monmouthcountyparks.com; 732.787.3033
Access: grounds, daily during daylight; house and exhibits expected to open in 2011. Parking: lot.

Heath Farm
219 Harmony Road (at Peace Lane, the informal driveway name)
Middletown, NJ 07748

The Heath Farm is an eclectic collection of buildings that honor the family of Clinton P. Heath, arguably Middletown's first noteworthy African American. The site also celebrates agriculture and provides a space for outdoor historical activities.

Formal public status of the site—the remaining holdings of Heath's daughter, Bertha, who spent her final decades prior to her death in 1998 at age ninety honoring her parents—began with the 1993 dedication of the Heath Memorial Garden, which was built around a gazebo, although the farm had been earlier used for various gatherings. Other buildings adjacent to the Heath residence were erected over the years as part of a lengthy project that Bertha entrusted to her nephew and Clinton grandson, Walter S. Spradley and his wife, Susie. Many of the exhibits relate to agriculture and Heath family heritage, but one is the remnant of another public collection. When the Seabrook-Wilson House (page 52) was emptied for transfer to the County of Monmouth, an effort was made to sort the Shoal Harbor Marine Museum's undocumented holdings to distinguish its collection from loans. After a protracted project to return borrowed items to their lenders, the remainder was transferred by the Township of Middletown to the Heath Farm and is on permanent exhibit. The 1999 opening to display the former

While the Heath Center can boast a number of exhibition buildings and a field for activities, its spiritual image is the Bob Mataranglo mural that depicts the life and times and family patriarch Clinton Heath. *Photo by Keith Maidlow.*

collection of the Spy House, to use the popular third name of the Seabrook-Wilson, was a major milestone of the Heath site.

The artistic highlight of the Heath Farm is the long mural by Monmouth County artist Bob Mataranglo that pictures Clinton Heath in his celebrated role as longtime gatekeeper of the Middletown crossing of the New York and Long Branch Railroad (now New Jersey Transit), completed in 2003. One of Heath Farm's more unusual buildings is the small replica of the first Clinton Chapel, an AME Zion church founded in 1890 by Clinton's brother, Calvin, which opened in 1894 at the Red Hill Road site of the present chapel. The older building was destroyed by an incendiary fire in 1966.

heathfarmtripod.com; 732.671.0566
Access: varies, June–August; at other times or by appointment, call and leave a message. Parking: street.

CHAPTER 2

RIVER REGION

COLTS NECK

Montrose School

13 Cedar Drive

Colts Neck, NJ 07722

The Montrose School, the only remaining Colts Neck one-room school in public ownership, provides object lessons for preservation and school financing, in addition to being a fine exhibition building.

The school at the western edge of the once rural township formerly known as Barrentown was built circa 1860—the circa 1812 date on the historical plaque should be ignored—when it was Montrose School District No. 5, the penultimate in Colts Neck, which was followed by nearby Robbins No. 5½. It remained in educational use until the early 1920s, as the township was late in consolidating its by then old, inadequate and unsafe small schools. Voters repeatedly rejected a new school until 1920. Consequently, following the opening of the then modern brick school on the south side of County Route 537, a short distance east of Highway 34, each of the one-room schools was sold.

George V. Illmensee Sr. gave the derelict Montrose School to the Colts Neck Historical Society for restoration in 1965. After a preservation project, the former school reopened as a historic site and was used for interpretation and a variety of meetings until it again became dilapidated and fell into disuse. The Colts Neck Historical Preservation Commission, a municipal body, rescued the building anew, followed by its donation by the historical

The Montrose School recalls a time when Montrose, now remembered only by a street name, was a section of Colts Neck. Then each neighborhood had its own one-room school, a practice ended by opening the consolidated school in 1922.

society to the township in 2003. After a multiyear restoration project, the school is once more devoted to historical interpretation.

There are two lessons to be learned from the Montrose School. Its two-decade use into the twentieth century demonstrates that public education must be adequately financed. In addition, the school's second period of disuse while a historic site shows the importance of continual care and maintenance in order to preserve historical properties.

Access: events; by appointment for groups. Parking: street.

EATONTOWN

Eatontown Museum (Read House)
75 Broad Street
Eatontown, NJ 07724

The Eatontown Museum, a reminder of the town's rural roots, stands amid other historical buildings in the borough's downtown. It is alternately known

While the Eatontown Museum's exterior suggests a late-nineteenth-century expansion, the building represents a number of additions made to a house with a likely eighteenth-century origin.

as the Read House for John Read, who owned the place in conjunction with his two wives between 1932 and 1977.

The house's eighteenth-century origins were revealed during work following the borough's acquisition in 1977. A section of interior framing was left uncovered to show the mortise and tenon joining technique and interior mud and straw lining. The house was expanded at unspecified times in both the nineteenth and early twentieth centuries. The contents of the house include a variety of artifacts and documents relating to the history of Eatontown.

The house is adjacent to the St. James Memorial Church (Protestant Episcopal) (NRHP 1978) and across the street from the former First Presbyterian Church, which is now the Eatontown Community Center.

732.542.4026
Access: last Sunday of the month; events; WOM. Parking: lot in rear accessed via Throckmorton Street.

FAIR HAVEN

Bicentennial Hall (NRHP 1975)
25 Cedar Avenue
Fair Haven, NJ 07704

A free Fair Haven African American settlement predated the circa 1850 formal organization of the village, but most of its physical presence has been obliterated by development and population change. Bicentennial Hall, the former Fisk Chapel AME Church, embodies the spirit of that community and, in its current incarnation, has become a boroughwide meeting place.

The former AME Fisk Chapel was given to the borough following the congregations' erection of a new church. Its move to this site in 1976 gave rise to its current name of Bicentennial Hall; it is a public meeting space that still resembles a church.

The earliest local black house of worship was an 1833 AME congregation that relocated to Red Bank after their River Road church was destroyed by fire in 1873. The AME Bethel Church, which was organized in 1858, built this church at 38 Fisk Street in 1882, renaming it for General Clinton B. Fisk in recognition of his financial and social beneficence to the African American community. He employed them on his nearby Rumson estate, provided assistance by financing home ownership and contributed substantially for this edifice. This building, which also functioned as an entertainment and cultural center for the local blacks, became inadequate for worship purposes. Consequently, a new church was built on its site and dedicated in 1976. The redundant building was donated to the borough for use as a community center and then relocated to its Cedar Avenue site after being cut in two and moved on trailers by legendary house mover Duffy Fisher. The former church was rededicated and renamed Bicentennial Hall on September 18, 1976, Fair Haven's Bicentennial Day.

The hall served as a venue for a wide variety of community events, which included the introduction of the author's first history of Fair Haven. However, deterioration, which stemmed from structural problems related to the move and deferred maintenance, resulted in the building's closure for most of the first decade of the twenty-first century. Rehabilitation aided by a number of grants was begun and then halted, but renewed efforts ongoing at publication project the reopening for the Fair Haven 2012 municipal centennial.

Borough offices: 732.747.0241
Access: under restoration at publication; street view. Parking: street.

World War I Memorial
751 River Road at the Northwest Corner of Fair Haven Road
Fair Haven, NJ 07704

A vast outpouring of public sentiment to honor the participants of and those lost to what had been thought to be the war to end all wars, but which later became known as World War I, followed its conclusion. Many monuments were made of stone, similar to their Civil War predecessors, but metal material had become a practical alternative. Fair Haven's monument, mounted in Memorial Park, is an example of what is likely the most symbolic

The *Spirit of the American Doughboy*, pictured shortly after its dedication, is admired for its vigorous pose. If you think you have seen it before, perhaps you have, as the E.M. Viqueney statue has been replicated many times. Two others stand in Monmouth County.

image of that conflict. It is the dominant monument in a setting that now honors all of the community's veterans.

The Fair Haven figure, *The Spirit of the American Doughboy*, was sculpted by Ernest Moore Viqueney, who was born in 1876 in Spencer, Indiana (died 1946), and was a veteran of the Spanish-American War. Local efforts to install a monument soon followed the end of the war, but fundraising delayed its installation until 1924. If you think you have seen this statue despite never having been in downtown Fair Haven, perhaps you have, as it was replicated many times following the artist's first one executed in 1921 when he was a resident of Americus, Georgia. Observe that the soldier is a man of action—he holds weapons and charges through barbed wire and tree stumps. This vigorous pose contributed to the popularity of this figure. Its material, typically of pressed copper, made it relatively inexpensive to produce, a second major factor contributing to the replication of the statue over one hundred times.

Broad community support enabled the purchase of the corner site for the park and the statue that cost $1,925. It was dedicated on August 16, 1924, when the statue was unveiled by Mrs. Edward Doughty, the mother of Christopher, one of two borough residents killed in action. A plaque lists the names of all who served, including the town's second battle casualty, Walter Grover. The other memorials erected at the site over the years typically commemorated veterans of later wars, but they also include a monument remembering the borough residents lost in the September 11, 2001 attack at the World Trade Center.

Other sculptors made statues that bear resemblance to the Viqueney model, which can confuse the viewer. The Viqueney Doughboy has been fabricated in other materials, including stone. Some possess variations in their image. Miniatures suitable for home display and for installation in lamps were made in great numbers. Outdoor sculpture maintenance is often a challenge for a variety of reasons. The restoration of the Fair Haven example in the mid-1990s included the replacement of missing pieces and cleaning. Several Viqueney replicas exist in New Jersey, including two in Monmouth County. The Belmar statue is located at Highway 35 and Seventh Avenue. The Matawan figure is at the entrance to their Monument Park. The Fair Haven example may offer the most convenient and accessible site to park and view.

Borough offices: 732.747.0241
Access: public park. Parking: street.

LITTLE SILVER

Parker Homestead (State Register Historic Places 1976)
235 Rumson Road
Little Silver NJ 07739

The Parker family's deep roots in the history of Little Silver, where an early section was called Parkerville, make it particularly fitting that their ancestral

The Parker Homestead, which commands a prominent spot on the north side of Rumson Road, awaits an audience, as the Borough of Little Silver prepares its role for public use.

homestead be dedicated as a community center for history and culture. Their tie to the land, which originated in the second quarter of the seventeenth century, endured until the 1995 death of Julia Parker, who bequeathed the remains of their farm and this house to the borough.

The prominence of the property and early efforts to preserve the house resulted in the borough receiving a preservation award from the Monmouth County Historical Commission in 2003, but the significance of the property, the desire to know its true past and the need to adopt a comprehensive master plan resulted in a recent study that revealed that the house's origin was a one-and-a-half-story section in the center that dates around 1725 during the residency of Peter Parker. The first expansion initially added a story and two rooms with a side hall addition to the east, perhaps built around the 1740s during the time of Peter's son, Josiah. This part was raised to two full stories, perhaps in that century's third quarter, when Josiah's son, William "Boatman Billy" Parker, lived there. The most significant change that gave the building its present image was the raising of the original one-and-a-half-story section to two stories in the early twentieth century. Lesser changes include lean-tos on both ends; the one on the east dates from the eighteenth century, while the nineteenth-century lean-to on the west was rebuilt in the early twentieth century.

The once vast farm was reduced over the years, but its diminished parts continued in agricultural use into the 1980s. Julia's passing marked an end to over three centuries of family occupancy. The tranquil grounds are open, while usage plans for the building are ongoing at publication.

Access: grounds only. Parking: lot.

Post Office Museum
Rear 480 Prospect Avenue
Little Silver, NJ 07739

The Little Silver Post Office Museum is distinguished as the only former post office in Monmouth County to serve as a museum. Thus it represents a distinctive adaptive use project.

The Little Silver Post Office was established in 1879 as a successor to Parkerville, which had been founded four years earlier. Its Church Street location was chosen for its close proximity to the headquarters of J.T. Lovett & Company, the nursery stock dealer with a national customer base. The firm was not only the greatest generator of mail but also built this office around 1904. Lovett served as postmaster for a spell. This structure fulfilled its postal function until replaced in 1956 by the present, larger office at 20 Church Street; it then began a second role as a retail location. After its site

When the diminutive Little Silver Post Office Museum was in active service, it handled the business of one of the region's major mailers, the J.T. Lovett Company, a nursery that had a national mail order business.

was needed for new construction, this building was moved on May 31, 1973, to the present location behind the borough hall. The Little Silver Historical Society was organized at the time to operate the local history museum, which contains a variety of artifacts on Little Silver history.

www.littlesilver.org
Access: first Saturday of the month. Parking: lot.

RED BANK

Count Basie Theatre (NRHP 2009)
99 Monmouth Street
Red Bank, NJ 07701

Red Bank had multiple show houses in the heyday of movie theatres, but this was the largest and most artistic. Today the theater, renamed for Red Bank's best-known favorite son, endures as a live entertainment venue and remains an impressive example from the golden age of motion picture theaters.

The Neo-Classical theater, designed by Newark architect William E. Lehman, opened in 1926 as the Carlton, changed from the initially planned "State," a name still visible on the façade's pediment. (Decades later, Lehman had a second Red Bank commission, the expansion of the library at 84 West Front Street.) When completed, the Carlton was the fifth motion picture theater in Red Bank and proved the longest lasting, enjoying a forty-seven-year run. It opened at the waning of vaudeville and at the cusp of film with sound, then called "talkies." While the Carlton was host to occasional vaudeville shows, the configuration of its stage area demonstrates that it was intended primarily as a venue for film. Developer Joseph Oschwald served a trio of investors that included the legendary Walter Reade. The Carlton, an immediate artistic success as a theater, benefited from management that sustained entertainment success by installing and updating modern systems. Motion picture exhibition ended on December 25, 1973, the day prior to the Carlton's sale to the Monmouth County Arts Council.

The arts council operated the theater for a variety of entertainment events for a quarter of a century, as it also served as a community cultural

The Count Basie Theatre is pictured in 1973, when still known by its original name, the Carlton. When completed in 1926, the Carlton was the finest of Red Bank's five theaters. The Count Basie gleams following a recent restoration.

organization. Having found the theater a long-term costly drain on time and finances, the council transferred the house to a separate nonprofit corporation, the Count Basie Theatre, Inc. The latter has operated the theater since while undertaking an extensive, costly and effective restoration divided into interior and exterior phases. The business operation has also seen renewed success, as the theater assumed production of a growing schedule of impressive performances of a wide variety.

Jazz and swing music icon William "Count" Basie, born in Red Bank on August 21, 1904, brought enduring recognition to his hometown with frequent performance of his popular song "The Kid From Red Bank." The theater has given lasting recognition to Basie through its renaming in his honor shortly after his April 26, 1984 death.

See the bust of Basie in the lobby, executed by noted New Jersey sculptor Brian Hanlon.

www.countbasietheatre.org; 732.842.9000
Access: performances. Parking: street.

Railroad Station (NRHP 1976)
195 Monmouth Street (at Bridge Avenue)
Red Bank, NJ 07701

The New York and Long Branch Railroad, a line that opened in 1875, transformed the region along its road, spurring industrial development, residential expansion and the growth of the resort industry; the nature of its impact varied depending on the town or area. Red Bank is a rare surviving station from the first year of operation, a large and artistic example built to reflect the importance of this stop. It remains as the best preserved of the original stations.

This road, the second rail line to come to Red Bank, followed the 1860 Raritan and Delaware Bay Railroad, which located its station nearby, a short distance to the north and east; their tracks crossed the New York and Long Branch just south of the latter's station. The newer railroad accentuated the Red Bank pattern of development where industry was clustered on its west, while its residential districts spread on the eastern part of town. While steamboats and other vessels provide glamorous accent to Red Bank history, transport on the Navesink River was often unreliable and slow, as the shallow

The Shingle-style Red Bank station retains its essential original appearance, as its surroundings have undergone change, including the erection of high-level platforms and the removal of its canopies.

river froze in winter and shoaled at any time. This station, which serves as a commuter hub, provides access to the city for travelers from a number of surrounding towns.

Nearby to the north, a similar station stands in Matawan. Both utilize a design that the Central Railroad of New Jersey, the builder of the New York and Long Branch, built on other lines. A tiny original station in Middletown has been adaptively used after replacement by a modern station in 1986. An artistic station dating from 1889 stands one stop to the south at Little Silver. It is a Richardsonian Romanesque building designed by Peabody and Stearns, although its design source is frequently misattributed to other architects.

Access: interior, generally weekday mornings, but the exterior has the historic value. Parking: street; lots are regulated for rail users.

Woman's Club of Red Bank (NRHP 1982)
164 Broad Street
Red Bank, NJ 07701

The Woman's Club of Red Bank occupies a residential reminder of the late nineteenth century when expansive estates lined upper Broad Street. While the grounds have shrunk since Anthony B. Reckless built his fine Italianate mansion in 1874, the preserved house remains one of the borough's premier landmarks.

The club traces its origins to the 1896 Round Table Coterie literary society, which changed its name the next year to Philomathian and became formally organized by 1916 and incorporated a year later. The local group joined the nationwide Greater Federation of Woman's Clubs and followed the federation's mission of improving communities through volunteer service. Local activity, particularly ambitious during the war years, included community health, social gatherings and literary events. The club began its work without a headquarters but seized the opportunity to buy the Reckless place in 1921. Its financial acumen permitted a substantial down payment and the ability to pay off the mortgage in only five years. At the time, upper Broad Street was still mainly a private-home residential development. However, the street's character would change in that decade, as Broad's commercial and multiple dwelling development edged south as its larger estates were broken up. The club rented upper-story rooms

The now lightly tinted Woman's Club, undergoing a fine restoration program, is pictured in the recent past with bunting celebrating an event. Its members have made the owner's name, Reckless, part of their image that reflects a heightened level of activism. *Courtesy of redbankgreen.com.*

to single professional and businesswomen but realized as the twentieth century waned that its membership was aging at a time when finances became a greater challenge. Its time-honored operational model would not endure. As members were aware that the house was a prime asset, the club attained National Register recognition, ended its residential role, obtained a preservation plan and began a long, extensive restoration project that is ongoing at publication.

The club was also revitalized by settling internal issues and attracting a younger, energized membership that redefined its mission to reflect contemporary community needs. They include a literacy program for local girls and cultural activity such as its Jazz and Blues Concert Series. Its home, the Reckless Estate, is a core element of members' identity, so much so that they call themselves "Reckless Women."

Another of upper Broad's former large estates was moved to a nearby location. The James B. Peters residence, which once adjoined Reckless, can be seen at 21 Peters Place, where it is adaptively used as an office.

www.womansclubofredbank.org; 732.747.7425
Access: events. Parking: street; lot in rear.

RUMSON

First Presbyterian Church of Rumson (NRHP 2010)
4 East River Road
Rumson, NJ 07760

Presbyterianism was a key faith in the early spiritual history of Rumson. Presbyterians took, in time, the original nondenominational church that was established by the founder of the Port Washington development, Thomas Hunt, in order to facilitate settlement of the area. It became the Oceanic section of the future borough. This extant early church structure

The rich Shingle-style exterior design of the First Presbyterian Church of Rumson by master architect Thomas Hastings urges a visit inside, where the scalloped interior shingling and the stained glass are equally impressive.

remains as the public building, Bingham Hall; this replacement is one of the ecclesiastical masterpieces of the shore.

The distinguished clergy, the Reverend Thomas Hastings, had a summer home on a multifamily Navesink River compound located east of Third Street, a tract that is best remembered for Matthew C.D. Borden, the New England fabric magnate who was one of the wealthiest men in America. Hastings was a regular guest preacher at the early Oceanic church. Presbyterian and other Rumson figures who had bought Hunt's church in 1855 organized the Oceanic Presbyterian Church in 1861 and then replaced their building with this magnificent edifice designed by the minister's son, also Thomas Hastings. This was an important early work of the architect, whose firm Carrere and Hastings became nationally renowned for numerous significant commissions. Those commissions included hotels, such as the Jefferson in Richmond, Virginia, and, locally, Lakewood's no longer extant Laurel-in-the-Pines; offices; and public buildings, notably the New York Public Library. The firm also designed the church's manse on the corner.

The Shingle style is an important and infrequent American-developed late nineteenth-century architectural style. Many of its finest artistic expressions are on eastern shore locales. The church's asymmetrical shape readily draws the eye, specifically to its octagonal dome, tower and port cochere. An inspection of the interior rewards the visitor by revealing rare, scalloped shingled wall cladding and a rich collection of stained glass that portrays biblical scenes. They were fabricated by four studios, including Tiffany of New York. Fellowship Hall, connected on the west, is a modern addition.

Nearby, the original church, now Bingham Hall, stands at 40 Bingham Avenue. After the building served various public incarnations after use as a church, the property was sold in 1956 to the Borough of Rumson. It is open for various community events, typically meetings, but the exterior and grounds are accessible. In addition, the Carrere and Hastings–designed carriage house/stable for the aforementioned Matthew C.D. Borden, now a private residence, is readily visible on the street at 68 West River Road. See also herein the Monmouth County Park System headquarters at Brookdale Farm, Middletown (pages 29–30).

www.rumsonpresbyterian.org; 732.842.0429
Access: worship; WOM. Parking: lot.

St. George's by-the-River Episcopal Church (NRHP 2007)
7 Lincoln Avenue
Rumson, NJ 07760

St. George's, founded in 1875, built its first church at the southeast corner of Bellevue Avenue and Ridge Road, a locale that gave rise to the tag "on-the Hill." The congregation was convinced to relocate, perhaps in an effort to establish a location closer to more members' homes, but for the most part, it was in response to the generous offer of Alice C., the widow of William Everard Strong, to build a memorial edifice following his May 14, 1905 death. Located at the edge of the Shrewsbury, this St. George was designated "by-the-River." The magnificent granite and limestone English Gothic structure was an early work of Walker and Gillette, a New York firm better known for its design of office buildings. Its cornerstone was laid September 25, 1907, which was followed by its consecration by Bishop Scarborough in June 1908.

A number of expansions of St. George's Church and the construction of connected related buildings have made the overall structures to form a close, or a piece of ground occupied by the church and its dependent buildings.

Also known in its early years as the Strong Memorial Church, St. George's added a parish center in 1908 and a rectory; both were connected to the main church by the 1946 construction of the cloisters, a series of classroom buildings that enciled the courtyard. In the 1950s, the chantry was added, a small place of worship within the nave, as was the Chapel of the Resurrection, an enclosed room behind the chantry. The church is also distinguished by the Mary Owen Borden Memorial Carillion, bought in England in 1934 and installed in the east tower, one of several gifts of major benefactor Bertram Borden. St. George's was listed on the National Register of Historic Places in 2007. The former church, which still stands at the aforementioned location, has been incorporated into the campus of the Rumson County Day School.

www.stgeorgesrumson.org; 732.842.0596.
Access: worship. Parking: street.

Seabright Lawn Tennis and Cricket Club (NRHP 1991)
5 Tennis Court Lane, at the Northeast Corner Rumson Road
Rumson, NJ 07760

The Seabright Lawn Tennis and Cricket Club has stature as the second oldest tennis club in America. In addition, it possesses a fine clubhouse, one designed by a distinguished New York firm, while members play on grass courts that are among the finest in existence. The tradition-bound organization was once a major stop on the United States tennis circuit.

For some years following the 1877 start of play at estate owners' courts and the club's formal organization the next year, games were played at a number of temporary locations. Then, in 1886, leaders of the group bought around nine acres on the eastern end of Rumson Road, a thoroughfare that had attained recognition as one of the finest country drives in America. They financed construction of the headquarters by the sale of gold bonds that offered a 6 percent return. The Shingle-style clubhouse with Tudor elements, designed by Renwick, Aspinwall and Russell, was built that year on the northwest corner of the lot.

A roster of early players here reads as a who's who of American tennis for the first half of the twentieth century. The list included Dwight F. Davis of Davis Cup fame; Holcombe Ward, a national amateur champion; and Bernon S. Prentice, the club's longtime guiding light who donated the

The fine long-rooted grass courts are a treasured part of the tradition that embodies one of the oldest tennis clubs in America, one that has earned National Historic Landmark stature. *Courtesy of Dorn's Classic Images.*

Prentice Cup, a trophy still in quadrennial competition by combined teams from Yale/Harvard versus Oxford/Cambridge. Another member, John Doeg, was a national singles champion. Changing travel patterns caused by the Second World War and the evolving nature of the tennis circuit resulted in a drop off of outside competitive events the postwar years. Club tradition has long-embraced and cherished its carefully nurtured turf, which has been for so long deeply rooted in members' values, that its maintenance was considered as far back as 1908 as a reason for not joining other single-sport organizations in the formation of the Rumson Country Club. The 1991 National Register listing was followed the next year by designation as a National Historic Landmark.

www.sltcc.org
Access: members and guests only, but prominent street view; WOM. Parking: Tennis Court Lane.

SHREWSBURY

Allen House (Monmouth County Historical Association) (NRHP 1974)
400 Sycamore Avenue
Shrewsbury, NJ 07701

The Allen House on the northwest of the historic four corners has undergone numerous incarnations over three centuries, while its interpretation by the Monmouth County Historical Association returns the place to its most significant: a colonial-era tavern, where it was the scene of a horrific event during the Revolution.

The building, begun around 1710 as a residence, was transformed in 1754 into a tavern by Josiah Halstead, a carpenter by trade, from which time it was known as the Blue Ball. The tavern in the eighteenth century typically also served as an inn, a place that was more than a watering hole, as many, including the Blue Ball, served as centers of community life.

The interior of the Allen House conveys the ambiance of an eighteenth-century tavern, the interpretation presented by its owner, the Monmouth County Historical Association. Also note the garden at the west end of the building.

Early New Jersey law mandated that towns establish and maintain taverns because they were critical for the protection of travelers as affording overnight places to stay. Safety was an issue, as the era's roads were often nonexistent and paths were often difficult to navigate. They were hardly inns of comfort, as lodgers were required to share beds with strangers, costs could be steep, the place dirty and the fare barely edible. However, they were typically the only accommodations, as the hotel as we know it did not gain traction until the early nineteenth century. Halstead's exertions earned his establishment the reputation as the area's best. Halstead stayed for two decades and then was succeeded by others. At the Blue Ball, a band of marauding Loyalists surprised a group of sleeping Continental soldiers in 1779, killed three and captured nine in a raid that would become known as the Allen House Massacre.

While the building was erected by Judah Allen, the Allen House namesake is 1814 co-buyer Dr. Edmund W. Allen, who was then the area's only physician but apparently not a relation. The place was expanded to include a store that operated for a century until destroyed by fire on April 17, 1914. The house was repaired, but not the store. A need to preserve the Allen House was recognized by the late 1920s after Margaret, the last Allen, sold it in 1927. The various occupancies that followed included an antique shop and tea room. The last private owners of the Allen House were Henry H. and Nellie Reid Holmes; she bequeathed the house to the association. After an early 1970s preservation project, the association fitted the main room as a colonial-era tavern, although absent the liquid refreshment and shared beds. However, the Allen House conveys the ambiance of period gathering places.

www.monmouthhistory.org; 732.462.1466
Access: 1:00–4:00 p.m. Thursday–Saturday, May–September; WOM. Parking: lot.

Christ Church (NRHP 1995)
380 Sycamore Avenue
Shrewsbury NJ 07702

The stature of Christ Church as Monmouth County's most important colonial house of worship stems from its age, design by the period's most significant regional architect, location in the heart of one of the county's two original settlements, its state of preservation and role in the community.

There are a number of burials under the floor of Christ Church, while its cemetery portrays centuries of funerary practice. Two noteworthy monuments are the Gillespie sarcophagus, south of the church, and the portrait of Edward C. Hazard in his monument by famed sculptor Daniel Chester French, located at the yard's northwest corner.

Its fine collection of historical documents and interior appointments make a visit particularly rewarding during a history event.

Christ Church, which dates its founding to the 1702 Christmas Eucharist celebrated at the Lewis Morris Tinton Falls residence, bought a 1.6-acre lot at the southeast of the Shrewsbury historic four corners of Sycamore Avenue and Broad Street. The congregation's first church, a brick structure, was erected here in 1732. Robert Smith (1722–1777) designed the present edifice, which was built between 1769 and 1774. The most notable features of the interior finishing are the two canopy-covered, seven-by-eight-foot box pews on the east end of the sanctuary. One was owned by the rector, while the second was reserved for important visitors. Once common in colonial churches, the Shrewsbury examples are rare survivors. The church's most visible change was the addition in 1874 of the ten-foot-square front tower, over which the original cupola was surmounted. The tower incorporates a three-face clock that was paid for by public subscription. Important interior changes from the early 1880s include the installation of the cut-crystal etched-glass chandelier, a carved altar of butternut wood, bronze communion railing, the eagle lectern and prayer stalls.

The more valuable items of the church's superb collection are rarely inside the church, such as the silver chalice and paten presented in 1738 to Christ Church by the Lord Chamberlain when the church received its royal charter. The pewter plate from that set is regularly on view, as is the elaborately carved oak Bishop's Chair from the 1860s and a rare Vinegar Bible, so named as a consequence of a printer's erroneous spelling in the parable of the vineyard. The parish, which maintains an active interest in celebrating its rich history, also holds an impressive collection of documents and photographs.

The present church was built over a portion of its early graveyard; early interments are recalled by three tombstones set in the floor of the present building. Its significant cemetery will enhance the visit, as it displays three centuries of funerary custom. While the viewer will have many choices for a favorite, the author suggests searching for the sarcophagus of major Christ Church benefactor George DeHaert Gillespie (1814–1884), just south of the rear of the church, and the stone of local industrialist Edward C. Hazard (1831–1905). The latter, located at the northwest corner of the lot, contains a fine stone portrait of the deceased that was executed by famed sculptor Daniel Chester French. History Day, typically the Saturday of the Weekend in Old Monmouth, is a notably rewarding time for a visit.

www.christchurchshrewsbury.org; 732.741-2220
Access: worship; events; WOM. Parking: lot.

The Presbyterian Church at Shrewsbury
352 Sycamore Avenue
Shrewsbury, NJ 07702

The Presbyterian Church at Shrewsbury regards 1732 as its founding, which is the year it believes its first church was built. The congregation was chartered in 1750, but they claim Presbyterian activity around Shrewsbury began as early as 1705, the year John Boyd was licensed as the first minister to be ordained by the first Presbytery in this country. Their deteriorated, early church was demolished at an unknown date. The group then worshipped elsewhere, including at Christ Church, for an unspecified spell before their 1821 undertaking to fund and build a new church, culminating in the dedication of the present Greek Revival edifice on September 29, 1822. The church retains its essential original form, although changes include the construction of the bell tower in the 1840s, the addition of a social room in

The Presbyterian Church at Shrewsbury, located adjacent to Christ Church, gives, for practical purposes, the borough five landmarks at its historic four corners.

1905 and the erection of the steeple in 1964. Blair Hall stands adjacent on the east, a 1977 replacement of an earlier hall that was destroyed by fire on February 2, 1974.

www.tpcas.org; 732.747.3557
Access: worship; events. Parking: lot.

Shrewsbury Religious Society of Friends (Quakers)
375 Sycamore Avenue
Shrewsbury, NJ 07702

Friends, or followers of the Religious Society of Friends, also popularly known as Quakers, were among the original 1665 settlers of Shrewsbury village. They established the first Friends Meeting in New Jersey, one that is also the state's earliest rural religious congregation. Their first meetinghouse was erected around 1672 about a mile from this spot, believed to have been in the vicinity of the present Little Silver railroad station. It was destroyed by an unknown cause, perhaps fire, circa 1690s. After the group purchased the northeast of Shrewsbury's historic four corners in 1689, they completed their first house of

The Religious Society of Friends, popularly known as the Quakers, is the oldest religious organization in Shrewsbury. This building dates from 1816, but the cemetery and their earliest house of worship were established in the seventeenth century.

worship here by 1703, which was destroyed by fire at an unspecified date. The early history is obscure, but some believe this 1703 building was replaced by one built of brick. A brick meetinghouse burned in 1810.

The present frame, wood timber construction meetinghouse was built in 1816. The space between the interior and exterior walls is filled with brick believed to have come from the earlier building. It is designed with the traditional Friends' two-cell interior that provides separate gathering spaces for men and women. Movable panels in the wall that separates the two spaces were closed for business discussions and kept open for access for worship and all other activities. An upper gallery has benches that extend around three sides of this building.

Friends worship in Shrewsbury has encountered difficulties and at least one spell of reduced activity. A circa 1828 schism that began in Philadelphia caused an Orthodox group to leave this site and establish a separate house of worship nearby on Broad Street, or Highway 35, a building that was later Library Hall and subsequently demolished. This existing building was retained by a liberal group known as Hicksites for their founder Elias Hicks, a Long Island farmer. The locals merged with the Manasquan Meeting in 1907 and traveled there, as the combined group used the Manasquan house as their principal place of worship. The unheated Shrewsbury building was used for some warmer weather worship and lectures. Its stature was recognized by documentation in 1940 by the Historic American Buildings Survey. After the Shrewsbury Meeting was reorganized in 1943, worship here has been continuous in a building that has been little changed. However, the need to repair 1968 fire damage in the east room was followed by a remodeling that included a fellowship hall, kitchen and restroom. An ancient cemetery with its oldest stone dating to 1714 is on the grounds. Visitors interested in a second Quaker site may wish to see the Manasquan Monthly Meeting, which has a circa 1886 meeting house at 2287 Meetinghouse Road, just off the Manasquan Circle at its northeast arc, at Highway 35 and County Route 524.

www.shrewsburyquakers.org; 732.741.4138
Access: worship; events; WOM. Parking: lot.

Shrewsbury Historical Museum (NRHP 1974)
419 Sycamore Avenue (Municipal Complex)
Shrewsbury, NJ 07702

The Shrewsbury Historical Society Museum is testament to the merits of the effective teaching of New Jersey history in the schools and the vision of its legendary founder, elementary school teacher J. Louise Jost. She expanded the activities of her Shrewsbury Boro School Jerseyana Club into a local history facility and, virtually single-handedly in its early years, built the museum and library that is enjoyed by the borough and a wider audience today. When this club disbanded, it donated accumulated artifacts to the newly organized society.

The museum is located on the premises of the borough's municipal hall, which was formerly housed in the two-and-a-half-story frame Wardell House. The site of the future museum was that property's carriage house, which was destroyed by fire December 12, 1976. Since insurance proceeds and a prospective $30,000 federal grant would not have been adequate to build any municipal facility that had then been under consideration, Miss Jost convinced the borough to apply those funds to a planned museum for which the historical society would raise the balance. The building, which was designed by Samuel Abate, opened in 1984.

The new museum rapidly built a collection of prints, documents, photographs, decorative arts and other artifacts that portrayed the history of the ancient settlement from seventeenth-century origins, through its

The as-built appearance of the Shrewsbury Historical Museum is harmonious with the early buildings of its surroundings, but an earlier rejected proposal had been a modern design.

1926 municipal organization into the recent past. Emphasis was placed on the old families and their houses that gave rise to the "Millionaires' Row" nickname (see Historic District, page 84), notably the Hazards who also had a condiments factory here that branded many products with the name Shrewsbury. Among the more compelling artifacts are three detailed scale models of the Allen House, Christ Church and the Presbyterian Church. The Hazard Collection, notably the albums of artistic labels, make local manufacturing come alive, while the Shrewsbury Boro School Collection gives more than a passing nod to its Jerseyana Club roots and the accomplishments of the students. The collection also pays respect to the town's ancestral namesake, Shrewsbury (pronounced Shrowsbury), located in Shropshire County, England. The aforementioned Wardell House is the common name for the circa 1825 residence built by Seth Lippincott. The house, which stands adjacent to the municipal hall next to the museum, was expanded perhaps in the early twentieth century. It was vacated when the new hall was completed, and it remains empty at publication. However, its historic stature is reflected by its entry on the National Register of Historic Places in 1974.

732.530.7974
Access: Saturday, 10:00 a.m.–2:00 p.m.; WOM. Parking: lot.

Shrewsbury Historic District (NRHP 1974)
Along Sycamore Avenue and along Broad Street
Shrewsbury, NJ 07702

The historic district embraces land on the sides of the historic four corners, extending in each direction. Three sites are individually listed on the National Register: Christ Church, the Wardell House and the Allen House, while the district itself was entered in 1974 for the inclusion of many well-preserved nineteenth-century and older houses that were owned as summer residences by wealthy city dwellers. There were sufficient numbers to give the Sycamore Avenue the designation "Millionaires' Row." The stretch of Sycamore west of Broad to the railroad is especially noteworthy as most of the houses have historic significance. Many houses east of Broad are also significant; particularly notable are 355, the Benjamin White house that dates to 1789; the former Presbyterian manse at 348; and no. 197, which has eighteenth-century origins, as well as others here from the late nineteenth and early twentieth centuries. The Edward C. Hazard condiments factory was just north of this stem. While celebrated historically, the thought of a factory in a fine residential district would bring widespread condemnation today. Shortly after the formation of the borough in 1926, Shrewsbury passed a zoning law—prior to the time land-use regulation was common—an action taken to preserve the environment around its better sections.

Access: public streets. Parking: municipal lot at 419 Sycamore; walk.

Tinton Falls

Crawford House
750 Tinton Avenue
Tinton Falls, NJ 07724

The Crawford House, an important property in the Tinton Falls Village Historic District, commemorates a significant old family long active in borough commercial and public life and offers an opportunity to contemplate Monmouth County's earliest major commercial operation.

The Crawford House provides public access to one of the county's most historic areas that at one time was its economic center, the Lewis Morris iron works. Here one can listen to the falls, and view them a few yards away, which gave Tinton Falls its name.

The house, built in two sections, was begun at an unknown date in the first half of the nineteenth century. It utilizes a Dutch-style framing system, which is one of the latest examples in the region. The older section is on the west, or the right, as the viewer faces a building that does not have a strict east–west orientation. The eastern third of the house was added sometime later in that century. The house prominently shows its Colonial Revival alterations from the 1920s, notably a columned porch, which will be the period of the borough's current restoration interpretation. Crawford business interests included cattle slaughtering and meat sale operations conducted here from outbuildings for about a century into the 1960s. Allen E. Crawford (circa 1898–1970) was active in public life as a tax collector and charter member and chief of the Tinton Falls Fire Company. His wife, Ruth (1905–1986), held positions of tax collector and municipal treasurer for forty-seven years, as she served both the borough and its predecessor Shrewsbury Township.

The grounds provide a venue for contemplating the locale's historical significance. When the Tinton Falls Village Historic District was entered on the National Register in 1977, some of its key sites were no longer extant. However, the district's stature stems from its vital importance to early Monmouth County. Consider that before any municipalities existed— they date from 1693—or even the 1683 formal organization of the county itself, in the 1670s Tinton Falls Village was at the core of Monmouth's most important venture, Lewis Morris's iron forge. Pine Brook, which powered early operations, runs at the edge of this site, while the much-altered falls are visible across the street. A former dam was destroyed, and the drop of the falls was reduced by physical changes. However, changed character of the falls notwithstanding, Monmouth business began here. The former mill at the opposite intersection is a replacement that likely dates from the early nineteenth century of a gristmill reportedly on the site since the 1670s. The Crawford exterior restoration was accomplished in 2007. While the opening date of the building will depend on completing the interior work that is ongoing at publication, the grounds are open for events or casual viewing.

Access: events. Parking: lot.

CHAPTER 3

SOUTH AND SHORE REGION

ASBURY PARK

Convention Hall and Paramount Theatre (NRHP 1979)
1300 Ocean Avenue
Asbury Park, NJ 07712

Convention Hall, along with its joined Paramount Theatre, is arguably Asbury Park's most significant secular building. The artful structure, which has hosted a vast variety of business, entertainment, sporting and exhibition events, is the center of the city's public life.

A mysterious but convenient fire destroyed the Fifth Avenue Arcade on June 2, 1927, a time while the city had been planning a replacement facility. Warren and Wetmore of New York were the architects for the sizable brick building that was planned and built to extend well over the ocean. They produced an eclectic design that quoted a number of late nineteenth-through early twentieth-century revival motifs, including Renaissance and Moorish. The new building, which was completed in 1930, experienced a substantial, unanticipated growth in its audience when the radio station that relocated there had a live, upfront view to broadcast the tragic 1934 *Morro Castle* maritime fire as it evolved on the ocean-going liner, which had become beached at the edge of the hall. On January 12, 1928, fire also visited the casino at the southern end of Asbury's boardwalk, which created the opportunity for replacement by another Warren and Wetmore design. Thus, their two projects were new bookends for the most significant stretch

This image of the west façade of what is arguably Asbury Park's most impressive building, the Convention Hall/Paramount Theatre, can be viewed in the shadow of the statue of founder James A. Bradley, which stands in the square across Ocean Avenue.

of the city's boardwalk. While Convention Hall has been skillfully restored in the years prior to publication, the casino, a largely steel and glass structure given over to amusement, has fared poorly. Neglect led to demolition of a substantial part.

The south side of Convention Hall is a fine spot to observe nearby places significant to Asbury Park history. The enclosure of famed seer Madam Marie stood a few feet away at the edge of the boardwalk. The well-known music venue the Stone Pony is three blocks south at 913 Ocean Avenue. The adjacent boardwalk structure, best remembered for the restaurant at the north end that housed the region's last Howard Johnson's, is Philadelphian John D. Fridy's artful design, which was built in 1961. Giuseppe Morretti's statue of Asbury Park founder James A. Bradley stands in the center of Atlantic Square. It was unveiled on June 29, 1921, only twenty-three days after Bradley died on June 6.

Access: events; retail and dining spaces; Parking: street; be careful to seek out not always visible pay boxes.

Library and Library Square
500 First Avenue
Asbury Park, NJ 07712

The Asbury Park Public Library traces its roots to the 1878 formation of a literary club headed by Helen, the wife of Asbury Park founder James A. Bradley. The group organized later that year as the Asbury Park and Ocean Grove Library Association. The library's early history is vague, but the cornerstone was laid in 1880, while construction, which began in 1881, proceeded slowly. The site consisted of lots donated by Bradley on the southwest corner of Grand and First Avenues. The new structure had multiple uses, as library occupancy was initially limited to a single room on the west. Two impressive stained-glass windows were installed. The first, located on the east wall, was a gift of George W. Childs of Philadelphia and Long Branch, made in memory of his friend, former president Ulysses S. Grant, who is pictured in its center. It was unveiled with appropriate ceremony on March 8, 1886. The second on the west wall quotes a poem by Henry Wadsworth Longfellow below an image of a burial at sea in a burning vessel of Viking god Balder the Beautiful.

Asbury Park, Monmouth County's oldest public library, contains two impressive stained-glass windows; one is a memorial to President Grant, while the second was fabricated in the New York Tiffany studio. The adjacent Library Square was planned to provide a gracious view for the planned main entrance to the city.

The window's design is attributed to Theodore R. Davis (1841–1894) and was fabricated in the New York Tiffany studio at an unspecified date. Davis was famed as an artist while serving in the Union army during the Civil War, was later employed by *Harper's Weekly* and spent his latter years in Asbury Park, where he resided and had a studio. Following an 1897 referendum, Asbury Park attained stature as one of the first established public libraries in New Jersey. The building, which may have been remodeled around 1900 or even completed then, was not totally given over to library use until 1915. Its building's exterior was compromised around 1930 when a tower east of the entrance, an adjoining gable and a chimney were removed.

Library Square, a central green space in the city and planned as a significant public park, is bordered on the south by Asbury Avenue, the principal thoroughfare to the beach area. It was designed with numerous specimen plants and shrubs. Its centerpiece is a memorial fountain to Frank Larue Tenbroeck (1857–1906), who after serving as Asbury Park's first and third mayor died at a young age of forty-nine. Ground was broken for the fountain in June 1912, according to the *Red Bank Register* of the twelfth of that month, and was presumably completed in the same year. The fountain had long been in a state of disrepair prior to restoration by the Asbury Park Historical Society and rededication on April 18, 2004.

www.asburyparklibrary.org; 732.774.4221
Access: open six days a week. Parking: street.

HOWELL

Howell Historical Society
Mackenzie House
427 Lakewood-Farmingdale Road
Howell, NJ 07731

The core of the MacKenzie House is believed to be a small "settler's cabin," a modest structure that was added to over the years. This house is symbolic of the agricultural and milling history of the township.

Although it is located on a major county secondary highway with an interstate a few yards away, a step inside the Mackenzie House can provide the visitor with vivid reminders of the Township of Howell's agrarian past.

The nearby gristmill that was once part of this tract was likely built by Obadiah Allen, who bought property in this locale in 1767 and retained it until 1809. His successor, James Lloyd, served as sheriff and was a member of a family active in political life. The mill passed through numerous owners throughout the nineteenth century, when it appeared that more than one likely added to the house. James and Jessie MacKenzie, who acquired the property in 1956, were the last private owners, as a MacKenzie donated the house to the township in 1982. The Howell Historical Society undertook a preservation program for the ten-room house, added a research library and brought in artifacts, all part of their public exhibition and education programs.

732.938.2212
Access: Saturday mornings; WOM. Parking: lot.

Ardena School Museum
Old Tavern Road
Howell, NJ 07732

The Ardena School Museum is a survivor from and a reminder of the era when the sprawling rural township of Howell had eleven one-room schools. Its standing in the Squankum area followed the posteducational travels of the building.

An earlier, smaller Ardena School built on the north side of the present County Route 524 east of Vanderveer Road was replaced in 1855 by this building, which served for instructional purposes until the large, fine Colonial Revival contemporary Ardena School was opened in 1939. When no longer needed as a school, this building was sold and moved to an East Freehold location, where it was adaptively used as a woodworker–cabinetmaker's shop. The Howell Historical Society purchased the building in 1973 and moved it back to Howell, placing it at a location opposite the municipal hall.

The Howell Historical Society's active interpretation program will enable the visitor not only to see a former one-room schoolhouse but also to experience the ambiance of education there.

The society has refitted the former school with furnishings and old educational materials that suggest the challenges of learning under the primitive conditions of the one-room school era, such as heat from a stove, an outhouse for a restroom and, prior to electric service, illumination from natural light, oil lamps or candles. A variety of historical displays, including photographs and memorabilia, depict much more of this spread-out school system in Monmouth's largest municipal territory, a township that still contains reminders of its agrarian past. In brief, nineteenth-century education is replicated here.

The Township of Howell municipal complex across the street merits examination as many of its structures were built as part of the Preventorium, a health facility that opened in 1912. Its purpose was to remove urban children that were thought at-risk to diseases of the time, notably tuberculosis, as exposure to the country air and lifestyle was thought to reduce the likelihood of contracting illness. The complex is not interpreted as a historic site, but the place, although little known as such, has stature as a public health landmark.

732.938.2212
Access: 1:00–4:00 p.m. last Sunday of month. Parking: lot.

Long Branch

St. James Chapel (Church of the Presidents) (NRHP 1976)
1260 Ocean Avenue
Elberon, NJ 07740

St. James Chapel was built at the cusp of a major transformation of the character of Long Branch. Located at the southern edge of Elberon, the former house of worship still universally known as the Church of the Presidents is the most significant historic structure in Long Branch. The construction of a chapel by a downtown congregation also reflects the economic, social and political chasm between the city's year-round population and its seasonal summer residents, the underlying issue behind its erection and the one that is dominant in the rise and fall of Long Branch as a resort. While the Church of the Presidents is not open at publication, it is Monmouth County's largest and most significant restoration project and

The St. James Chapel, popularly known as the Church of the Presidents, is one of Monmouth County's largest and most ambitious restoration projects. Emerging visible signs of progress can enable the visitor to measure progress. Its locale on Ocean Avenue and street parking facilitate the visitor's viewing.

its preservation work has been done in stages that afford the visitor a look at ongoing progress. It has a prominent view from the street,

The origin of the edifice is a Shingle-style design by the noted New York firm Potter and Robertson, built in 1879. The prominent square tower was part of a fifteen-foot addition to the chancel designed by John B. Snook and Sons of New York and built in 1893. The church functioned as a summer chapel, which precluded the necessity of nearby residents to travel to the main location of St. James on Broadway. By the 1920s, the chapel was in precarious financial condition, as support by its wealthy following fell with fading finances and lessened use, culminating in St. James Chapel's deconsecrating in 1953 and sale for historical use. Edgar Dinkelspiel spearheaded the adaptive use and made the place a center of Long Branch historical and artistic activity, but he failed to build an organization that consequently led to the structure's precipitous deterioration. After his death in 1997, Edgar's widow, Florence, carried on, and finally sought outside help to rescue a by then dilapidated building, accomplished by the 2001 reorganization of the Long Branch Historical Museum Association. The association added numerous historical and community activists who had the foresight, energy and fundraising acumen to adopt and carry out in phases a preservation plan that is returning the structure to viability.

More research will be helpful to cement the elusive seven presidential associations with the chapel, as the claims lack specificity. The first substantive presidential tie was a memorial tablet mounted in June 1882 to honor the slain James A. Garfield, who died in the Francklyn cottage across the street. With respect to the other presidents, the chapel postdates the administration of Grant, who is known to have attended both this chapel and the St. James main church but reportedly regularly worshiped at the Centenary Methodist Church during his presidency. Wilson, the last of the seven and son of a prominent Presbyterian minister, has a commemorative plaque at the main St. James to mark his having attended an event there rather than the chapel. McKinley was rarely in Long Branch during his presidency. Harrison's visits were largely after his term in the White House, while Hayes and Arthur, who were regular hotel visitors to Long Branch, are known to have visited the chapel.

www.churchofthepresidents.org
Access: street view of restoration scene. Parking: street.

Elberon Memorial Church
70 Lincoln Avenue
Long Branch, NJ 07740

This Presbyterian house of worship was built as a memorial to Moses Taylor by his widow, Catherine A. Taylor. Moses died in 1882 after having attained stature as one of the gilded age's greatest industrialists. Taylor was a major financier whose varied career was highlighted by his control of the Delaware,

The exterior of Elberon Memorial Church, which is prominent on a quiet residential street, is always readily accessible, but the congregation meets only at 11:00 a.m. in the summer, when its ambitious and acclaimed music program can be experienced.

Lackawanna and Western Railroad at a time when that line was one of the most profitable in America.

The church is simply the best-preserved building from Long Branch's period of greatest significance. Its artistic design and rich, fine stained glass are an enduring testament to not only Taylor's power and wealth but also to the stature of Long Branch when it was arguably one of the east's most prestigious seashore resorts. While Elberon Memorial's prominent position on the street readily permits an exterior inspection, access to the inside is limited, as it is a summer congregation. The finely finished interior and the church's ambitious music program will make the effort to visit rewarding. Its fine pipe organ was built in 1885 by famed organ builder Hilbourne L. Roosevelt.

Identification of the architect has been disappointingly elusive. While investigation has centered around the practitioners for Taylor's other building ventures, confirmation of his identity is lacking. Still, the high artistic attainment of design and music prompted the author to have earlier referred to the place as "more than a church, Elberon Memorial is a community cultural treasure."

Access: 11:00 a.m. worship, summer only; prominent street presence. Parking: street.

MANASQUAN

Glimmer Glass Bridge (NRHP 2008)
Brielle Road over Glimmer Glass Creek
Manasquan, NJ 08736

The Glimmer Glass Bridge looks like an antique—which it is—but the bridge is distinguished for its rare engineering, the only example in New Jersey of a rolling counterweight cable lift bascule bridge.

The Glimmer Glass Bridge, built around 1898, uses technology developed by the French in the eighteenth century. The lift is operated by employing "a curved track and rolling counterweights where the work expended in raising the leaf is equal to the energy released by the falling counterweight," as it is described in A.G. Lichtenstein & Associates' historic bridge survey. An earlier example built on a New Jersey railroad is no longer extant. The bridge's rarity, which likely extends for an area some distance beyond New Jersey, justified its inclusion on the National Register of Historic Places. The bridge has been rebuilt over the years, but the span works are original. The bridge, which needs to be upgraded, is threatened since the Federal Highway Administration and the New Jersey Department of Transportation

Community activism and the securing of National Register listing helped preserve the Glimmer Glass Bridge after its planned replacement by a modern structure was announced. This view can be obtained from the apartment house parking lot on the Manasquan side. Be wary of gulls dropping clams here in order to break them for consumption.

have adopted a "no movable span" bridge policy, but an ardent community effort is ongoing to save this historical artifact of bridge engineering.

Access: public thoroughfare. Parking: not applicable; apartment house lot on the Manasquan side offers a brief view.

United States Life Saving Station No. 9 (NRHP 2008)
124 Ocean Avenue
Manasquan, NJ 08736

The Squan Beach Station, Monmouth's southernmost of the maritime rescue buildings that were spaced about three and a half miles apart along the state's shore, represents an important building type. Its size and condition reflect its fine prospects for adaptive use.

The present structure is a Duluth-style building erected in 1903 as a replacement for an 1872 structure. The design, developed by United States Life Saving Services architect George R. Tolman, is named for the locale of its first example, Duluth, Minnesota. The building, which later served as the Manasquan Coast Guard Station, was decommissioned in 1996 and given to the Borough of Manasquan in 2000. A maritime museum is planned for the ground floor, while community rooms may be located upstairs. The tower offers a fine view of the surrounding area.

Access: undergoing restoration at publication. Parking: street.

The Manasquan Station will be the largest of Monmouth's former lifesaving stations that will be open to public use. Restoration is underway at publication.

MONMOUTH BEACH

United States Life Saving Station No. 4
(State Register Historic Places 1999)
Monmouth Beach Cultural Center
128 Ocean Avenue
Monmouth Beach, NJ 07750

Two of Monmouth's four surviving lifesaving stations are described herein, this one and the southernmost at Manasquan. A third that remains at Sandy Hook is now used as its visitor's center, while a fourth is threatened. A variety of cultural and community events draws the visitor to Monmouth Beach.

The horrific toll of maritime disasters off the New Jersey shore, which had earned it the dubious distinction and nickname as the "Graveyard of the Atlantic," was even more heart wrenching when many of them were in view of witnesses on shore who were unable to provide assistance. Dr. William A. Newell's seeing thirteen mariners drown in 1839 while attempting to swim three hundred yards to Long Beach Island motivated

The image on this circa 1910 postcard is readily recognizable and enables the visitor to the cultural center to realize that the large exhibition room was once the area where the boats and major apparatus were stored at the now removed doors on the right.

him to convince Congress to establish the United States Life Saving Service ten years later. The northernmost, designated No. 1, was built in 1849 at Sandy Hook. Others were built about three and a half miles apart. Monmouth Beach, designated No. 4, was also established that year; its original building was near the ocean. A replacement was reportedly built in 1874 and the present structure in 1895, a time when it was relocated to the west side of Ocean Avenue.

The New Jersey Marine Police occupied the building in the 1960s but withdrew after the ravages of the December 11, 1992 northeaster. The vacant building was close to being demolished in 1999 when saved by a last-minute community effort; this group opened the Monmouth Beach Cultural Center the next year. While not interpreted as a historic site, the center lines its walls with historical images and demonstrates that historic structures can receive a second life compatible with their historic past.

Website not accessible at publication; 732.229.4527
Access: events; exhibitions. Parking: lot.

NEPTUNE (OCEAN GROVE)

The Great Auditorium
The Ocean Grove Camp Meeting Association
21 Pilgrim Pathway
Ocean Grove, NJ 07756

The Great Auditorium is the most impressive structure in Ocean Grove, one of the most significant buildings in Monmouth County and likely the largest frame building in New Jersey.

Spiritual enrichment and gathering among clergy and laity were fundamental not only to the Methodist founding of Ocean Grove but their camp meeting sites elsewhere as well. This practice elevated meeting venues to places of special significance; none is greater than the Great Auditorium. Designed by Fred Camp of New York, the Great Auditorium was built in 1894 over only ninety-two working days. It was the fourth structure on a site where first was built a modest octagonal preacher's stand. The building's size, which covers nearly six-sevenths of an acre, conveys impressive numbers, including a length of 225 by 161 feet wide, a 55-foot-high ceiling and an

The Great Auditorium, New Jersey's largest frame building, is imposing on the exterior, but a step inside and a view of its extensive seating provides an intimate view of the grandeur of the interior. Come for a summer organ or other concert.

east tower 131 feet high. Its seven main trusses, placed 21 feet apart, have 161-foot spans. The seating capacity of 6,500 is now fewer than its former 10,000, with the reduction having stemmed from the replacement of wood chairs with theater seats.

The building's functioning operates at a high degree of efficiency. Its wood interior enhances acoustics. Neither heated nor air conditioned, its 262 windows and doors help maintain comfort through breezes that sweep through doors and circulate out through balcony windows. Safety has been enhanced through later installation of an automatic sprinkler system. For visitors' patriotic stirrings, the flag on the wall behind the stage that is lit by sequentially blinking bulbs, which make it appear to wave, is an enormous crowd pleaser. The 125-rank Hope Jones organ built in 1907, which is regarded as one of the finest in America, is an instrument that possesses musical stature as great as that enjoyed by the building. Indeed for some, the free summer organ concerts are the highlight of their visit to Ocean Grove.

Many famed preachers, musical figures and United States presidents have been featured in the Great Auditorium. Nearly every New Jersey governor has appeared here. It is the central gathering space in the Grove for a variety of events, but the grandeur of the place can be appreciated just by walking through the empty building. While the building has religious origins, its long use for a variety of secular gatherings has given the Great Auditorium an additional public identity, one that should preclude any "establishment issue" for future public use.

www.oceangrove.org; 732.775-0035
Access: events in the summer; tours, as available in season; casual walk-in visits.
Parking: street.

Historical Society of Ocean Grove
Centennial Cottage
McClintock and Central Avenues
Ocean Grove, NJ 07756

Elizabeth Fell built this Stick-style summer cottage in 1879 at 47 Cookman Avenue. The style, characterized by vertical building members, was often called Swiss Chalet during its period of fashion on the shore in the

The Centennial Cottage is the only Stick-style house open to the public in Monmouth County. The donor who gave it to the Historical Society of Ocean Grove acquired the building in 1969, Ocean Grove's centennial, ergo its name.

1860s–80s. This example is richly decorated with vergeboard. The Robert Skolds acquired the place and in 1969, the one hundredth anniversary of the founding of Ocean Grove, and donated the house to the Camp Meeting Association. After the cottage was moved nine blocks to its present location, the historical society restored and opened it for exhibition purposes to portray life at the shore in the late nineteenth century. The earliest of the society's museum exhibitions were shown here. However, in time the growing collection required its own facility as is described in the following entry.

Museum

50 Pitman Avenue

Ocean Grove, NJ 07756

The historical society's rich collection of artifacts, photographs, documents and books that are housed behind an inauspicious storefront can tell the complete history of Ocean Grove through exhibitions that are delights to the eye.

An inauspicious storefront contains a wealth of artifacts, documents, memorabilia, books and pictorial history relating to Ocean Grove. Changing exhibits merit repeated visits.

Ocean Grove was the earliest section of the Monmouth shore south of Long Branch that became intensively active in the post–Civil War expansion of leisure time and travel opportunities. It was founded in 1869; that date and the society's telephone number reinforce the memory of both. Consequently, an enormous output of souvenirs, memorabilia, photographs and other ephemera was produced for the Grove and its thousands of visitors. A comprehensive representation found a home here. One can obtain a meaningful preview of the museum from home by accessing the society's website, which includes a fine online selection of their collection.

Both locations: www.oceangrovehistory.org; 732.774.1869
Access: summer seasonal hours; WOM. Parking: street.

Ocean Grove Historic District (NRHP 1976)
Entire town

All of Ocean Grove was designated a historic district as a consequence of its design and the fine state of preservation of most of its Victorian period buildings, both religious structures and residences. It is a compact area in which the entirety can be accessed by foot in a setting that is a walker's delight.

Ocean Grove was selected by Methodists as the site for their shore camp meeting grounds for the salubrious qualities of the local environment, notably the absence of mosquitoes; it was founded in 1869. All of the property is owned by the Ocean Grove Camp Meeting Association, which offers long-term leases to the owners of the buildings. The Grove was laid-out behind a half mile of beachfront with a plan whereby the lots near the shore were set back to facilitate the flow of air and breezes through the interior. The blocks behind the shore were broken up by squares and parks. Most of the Grove's buildings were erected during the latter third of the nineteenth century and embrace the styles current in the late Victorian era. A great majority remain well preserved. A small business district is in harmony with its surroundings, while the Grove's many small hotels and former lodging places strive to keep current with changing times and tastes.

Tents of the portable variety provided shelter for early visitors. The tenting tradition is continued through permanent structures that have fixed frame rears, while the fronts are hung with canvas tenting that is erected at the start of the summer season and stored offsite during the off season.

Their number has been reduced over the years, but the remaining 114 tents rarely change lessees.

The premier meeting and religious structure, the Great Auditorium, is described separately (page 100). The 1877 Bishop Janes Tabernacle and the 1887 Thornley Chapel are fundamental to Methodist activity at the Grove and also merit a visit. Ocean Grove, which received a legislative charter in 1869, is part of the Township of Neptune. The locals attempted to establish a separate borough in 1920, but their nascent effort was ruled unconstitutional the next year.

Information may be obtained from the historical society.
Access: public streets. Parking: street.

OCEAN TOWNSHIP

Township of Ocean Historical Museum Association
Eden Woolley House
703 Deal Road
Oakhurst, NJ 07755

The Township of Ocean Historical Museum Association and the township itself relocated a derelict historic house that stood on a nearby site that had been slated for development, undertook its preservation and subsequently accomplished one of Monmouth County's greatest restoration and adaptive use projects. The building is open as a local history museum, one that commemorates the memory of its significant former owner and exhibits a variety of historical subjects.

The house's mid-eighteenth-century origin is the one-and-a-half-story section on the east, or right as one faces the building. The association's records indicate that it was built by Thomas Woolley on property first acquired by the family via John Woolley's 1697 purchase. The two-and-a-half-story main block was built by Eden Woolley, perhaps the most prominent of the Woolleys, whose varied career included roles as farmer, businessman, surveyor of roads and, following the organization of the Township of Ocean at its 1849 split from Shrewsbury Township, membership on the new municipality's first township committee. The

The Eden Woolley House, now the Township of Ocean Historical Museum, is one of the county's greatest preservation successes. After relocation down Deal Road from a lot at the highway, it was transformed from a wreck to a gem.

house, which remained in the Woolley family until 1926, stood on the northeast corner of Highway 35 and Deal Road.

The museum association, founded in 1983 in conjunction with a new museum then located in part of the former Oakhurst School, counts the Township of Ocean Historical Society that was formed in 1970, as an antecedent. The group collected and exhibited at that 163 Monmouth Road location until the present building was opened.

The Eden Woolley House became available when its lot needed to be cleared in anticipation of commercial construction. It was given to the township by the developer with the provision that the building be relocated, which was accomplished in 2005 by moving the house by truck several hundred yards east on Deal Road. The enormous amount of work needed took years of effort by the volunteer organization, with township assistance, and resulted in a renewed structure that retained its integrity while meeting contemporary code. The association maintains the building as the main showpiece for a project that was so extensive and well done that the author believes that only those who saw it in its derelict condition can fully appreciate the magnitude of the group's accomplishment. In addition to permanent exhibits, exhibition space for changing historical displays will provide incentives for repeat visits. To build a wider audience and to extend their mission to embrace Ocean's historical boundaries, museum exhibitions include the several now separate municipalities that were formed from the original township. The author believes this step sets the local groundwork for the historical background of the emerging public issue of municipal consolidation.

The grounds, which are adjacent to the township library, include a 1915 children's playhouse that was erected by New York lawyer Joseph T. Ryan for his daughter, Rosemary, on the Wickapecko Drive estate he built in 1909. The playhouse was given to the township for removal when the estate grounds were sold for development in 1985.

At publication, the association is undertaking preservation of a circa 1900 water tower, a type of structure that once dotted the landscape but one that has become rare due to the lost utility of such structures. It is a survivor from the Haupt estate once on these grounds.

www.oceanmuseum.org; 732.531.2136.
Access: Tuesdays and Wednesdays, 1:00–4:00 p.m.; Thursdays, 1:00–4:00 p.m. and 7:00–9:00 p.m.; first and second Sundays, 1:00–4:00 p.m.; WOM Parking: lot.

SEA GIRT

Sea Girt Lighthouse
9 Ocean Avenue, at Beacon Boulevard
Sea Girt, NJ 08750

Several years' planning preceded the 1895 beginning of construction of the lighthouse at Sea Girt, which was needed to fill the long gap in shore navigational aids from Barnegat, on the northern tip of Long Beach Island, to Twin Lights, Highlands. This lighthouse, which was illuminated by a fourth-order Fresnel lens that flashed every six seconds, was placed into operation in December 1896. The two-and-a-half-story building, which has a three-story tower with walkway, appears at street level to be a residence of its period—which it was, in part, housing the light's keeper. A radio fog beacon was installed in 1921. The facility was operated by the United States Coast Guard during the early 1940s when its wartime role included keeping watch for German submarines. In 1945, after the lighthouse was considered

In addition to its light, the Sea Girt Lighthouse is distinctive by brick construction that stands out in a neighborhood of frame residences.

unneeded, it was decommissioned, and in 1956 after an expected sale to the State of New Jersey was not consummated, it was sold to the Borough of Sea Girt for $11,000.

After housing various community facilities, including a library, the costly-to-maintain building was leased in 1981 to the Sea Girt Lighthouse Citizens Committee, which restored the building and opened it for exhibition purposes. While other New Jersey shore lighthouses are taller or more architecturally distinctive, the combination of residential character with maritime beacon gives Sea Girt a special appeal to its ardent boosters.

www.seagirt-nj.com/seagirtlighthouse; 732.974.0514
Access: Sundays, 2:00–4:00 p.m., early May to Sunday before Thanksgiving, except holiday weekends. Parking: street.

National Guard Militia Museum
Sea Girt Avenue and Camp Drive
Sea Girt, NJ 08750

After a trial use at nearby Manasquan in 1884, the next year the State of New Jersey leased about 100 acres of the former Commodore Robert Stockton

Which does one see first at the National Guard Militia Museum, the informative exhibitions inside or the military vehicles and airplanes on the lawn? Both will satisfy.

estate then owned by the Sea Girt Land Improvement Company, to open the National Guard Camp at Sea Girt. The state acquired the property several years later, but their acquisition, apparently by condemnation, is lost to history. Their presence continues to date on a tract that has expanded to about 168 acres. The National Guard Militia Museum of New Jersey, founded in 1980, is housed at the southern end of that expanse in a former military building with a varied past that at one time included a drill hall. The museum's permanent exhibits commemorate and honor the history of the citizen-soldier, one that spans over two hundred years, a timeline that originated in our colonial period and continues now in the Mideast conflict. Changing temporary exhibitions add topicality to the permanent display.

Uniforms, some on dressed mannequins, some old and rare, effectively symbolize soldiers over the centuries; they engage the eye upon entering the main exhibition hall. A wide variety of artifacts and documents tell the story and varied roles of the state's forces. A vast warehouse space houses scores of weapons and military vehicles of varied description and age. One of the most fascinating exhibits here gives a nod to naval warfare and the perilous trials of early submarines. The twenty-nine-foot-long, twenty-ton wrought-iron vessel named *Intelligent Whale* was conceived during the Civil War and built and tested in that era. The vessel was bought by the navy, which conducted its own tests, a venture that presented great risk to the crew. They and the submarine survived, the lack of success of its sea trial notwithstanding. Experimental submarine vessels had a long history prior to their active naval operation; *Intelligent Whale* was not a successful one. The ship was displayed at the Brooklyn Navy Yard until it was moved to the Washington Navy Yard in 1968 and subsequently relocated to Sea Girt in 1999. The museum also conducts an acclaimed extensive oral history program that has captured the military memories of hundreds of veterans. If the building is not readily identifiable as a museum, the tanks, vehicles and aircraft in the field opposite let the visitor know he has arrived. One, an F-84F Thunderstreak, acknowledges Cold War European active service of the New Jersey Air National Guard. An even more impressive aircraft here is the F4D Phantom fighter, a plane that was utilized extensively by three service branches during the Vietnam War. Adult visitors need to show valid picture identification at the base gate on entering, such as a driver's license. The National Guard Militia Museum has increased its public profile in recent years but remains one of Monmouth County's best historical "secrets." The visitor is well advised to help them lose that status.

www.nj.gov/military/museum/index.html; 732.974.5966
Access: Tuesday–Thursday, 10:00 a.m.–3:00 p.m.; weekends, intermittent (call); events; WOM. Parking: lot.

SPRING LAKE

St. Catharine Church
214 Essex Avenue
Spring Lake, NJ 07762

St. Catharine Church, which is indisputably Monmouth County's most artistic house of worship, was built by benefactor Martin J. Maloney as a memorial to his daughter, Catharine, who died at sea in 1900 at age seventeen after a health-inspired pilgrimage to Europe. The Beaux-Arts–Classical Revival exterior is imposing; the interior, awe-inspiring.

The congregation now known as St. Catharine-St. Margaret traces its beginnings to the 1880 celebration of mass at a nearby hotel, worship that culminated in the 1882 founding of St. Anne's (the period spelling of today's St. Ann). They utilized the office of Patrick Charles Keely, the prolific Catholic architect of the late nineteenth century, to build a small church at Monmouth and Fifth Avenues. Maloney's love of God, devotion to his Catholic faith and generosity to the church are the background to his building a church as an expression of his grief. He promptly hired Horace

The architectural masterpiece St. Catherine Church, which embraces both the Classical Revival and Beaux-Arts styles, is Monmouth County's artistic twentieth-century house of worship. The richly decorated interior is awe-inspiring.

Trumbauer to design this edifice. The architect attained fame for country estates, including Shadow Lawn II (page 122), but he also designed Duke University and a number of public buildings. He previously worked for Maloney to design his Spring Lake Neo-Georgian mansion Ballingarry. After Trumbauer completed plans for an edifice in the shape of a Greek cross in October 1900, the cornerstone was laid on March 17, 1901, which was followed by the church's consecration on May 25, 1902, although construction continued into 1907. The church renamed itself St. Catharine in 1901 as recognition of Maloney's generosity.

The richly decorated interior of St. Catharine began with Maloney's 1904 commission of Gonippo Raggi (1875–1959) to come from Rome to execute over two dozen frescos and canvasses that reflect Maloney's love of and inspiration from art in the Vatican. This lengthy project was undertaken in two phases; the second was completed in 1928. Stained glass was executed by the famed Munich studios of Mayer and Company. The statuary and carved stonework was sculpted by Florentine sculptor Puggi. Maloney made many benefactions to Catholic causes and enjoyed a close tie to the Vatican, which honored him with the titles of papal marquis and papal chamberlain.

The extensive artistic and architectural splendors of St. Catharine cannot be done justice in a brief account. Visitors now will see the rewards of the church's extensive exterior and interior preservation projects of recent years, work that included removal of the dome's familiar green patina. St. Margaret was built in 1930 at Third and Ludlow Avenues to accommodate the need of an expanding Catholic population. The former St. Ann, after use by another congregation, was demolished. A Maloney daughter had Ballingarry razed in 1953 after an unsuccessful attempt to find a buyer. Maloney, his wife, Margaret, Catharine and other relatives are entombed in the family crypt beneath the Sacred Heart Chapel on the north side of the nave.

www.stcatharine-stmargaret.com; 732.449.5765
Access: worship; WOM. Parking: street.

Church of the Holy Trinity (NRHP 1991)
301 Monmouth Avenue
Spring Lake, NJ 07762

The Church of the Holy Trinity, Spring Lake's oldest house of worship, which was completed in 1881, is a fine, well-preserved example of Stick-style Gothic architecture.

Holy Trinity's establishment by wealthy Philadelphia summer residents reflects Spring Lake's settlement pattern. The groundbreaking on September

Located in proximity to the lake and the town's better-known churches, one could say that Trinity Episcopal is hidden in plain view. The summer congregation owns a little-known gem that is one of the shore's secret treasures.

17, 1880, was followed by the start of construction the next January and the first service on July 2, 1881. Episcopal bishop Scarborough was present at the dedication. The interior, richly finished in wood and decorated with stained glass, is intimate, moving and even precious. It is well worth a visit on the infrequent opportunities to enter.

www.holytrinityspringlake.org; 732.449.5240
Access: summer worship; events. Parking: street.

Spring Lake Historical Museum
423 Warren Avenue
Spring Lake, NJ 07762

Spring Lake, which was organized in the late nineteenth-century as a Philadelphia resort, grew with numerous hotels and elaborate summer mansions that covered the region near the ocean. The museum, located on the second floor of the borough's municipal hall, commemorates the history of an area informally known as the Irish Riviera through permanent and changing exhibits drawn from a large collection of artifacts, documents and photographs.

The institutional appearance on the exterior reflects the building's principal function as the borough's municipal hall, while the Spring Lake Historical Society's museum inside portrays vividly the rich history of one of the brightest spots on the New Jersey seashore.

Within the borders of Spring Lake, which possesses one of Monmouth County's finest-built environments, time and changing taste in vacation destinations have altered much of the Monmouth shore's lodging industry, having taken away Spring Lake's great hotels. One, the Essex and Sussex, survives after residential adaptive use. Many of the town's elaborate houses from the late nineteenth and early twentieth centuries remain, while several have become the more intimate bed-and-breakfast types of guesthouses. Two of the town's fine churches are separately described herein. Historical society exhibits capture the colorful past of Spring Lake's golden age.

Historical society events include periodic house tours. As the compact borough is readily seen on foot, the pedestrian can be assisted by the society's online walking tours. Indeed, the town is a walker's delight. Look for the nearby Tudor Revival 1923 Community House at Third and Madison Avenues, which houses the Spring Lake Theatre Company, the Spring Lake Library and Women's Club. The 1930 First Aid Squad Building (NRHP 1998) at 311 Washington Avenue is of historical interest as arguably the earliest separate first aid building in America.

Borough's website www.springlake.org/historical; 732.449.0772
Access: see site for details of seasonal Thursday morning and Sunday afternoon hours or call for appointment; events. Parking: street.

WALL

Information Age Science/History Learning Center (Camp Evans)
(NRHP 2002)
2201 Marconi Road
Wall, NJ 07719

The Information Age Science/History Learning Center, commonly known as InfoAge, located at the former Camp Evans area of Fort Monmouth, is important not only as the local heir of the fort's electronic military discoveries but also as a site for pioneering international wireless communications. At publication, the sprawling facility houses a consortium of museums, while ongoing restoration will expand a burgeoning operation.

The site's scientific origins began with famed inventor Guglielmo Marconi's 1912 purchase of rural farmland to establish his Marconi

Camp Evans, while remembered in the recent past as a unit of Fort Monmouth, is on a site founded by Guglielmo Marconi for wireless telegraph transmission. His workers were housed in the large brick building still known as the Marconi Hotel, but which now contains a group of museums organized by the Information Age Science/History Learning Center. Also see scientific instruments on site.

Wireless Telegraph Company of America for transatlantic radio communications. His early structures included four tall communications towers that ranged upward of four hundred feet high. A number of his operations buildings are extant including the large prominent brick building that housed his workers, a place still nostalgically called the Marconi Hotel. After the United States Navy took over the facility during World War I, it was returned to the company that later became part of the Radio Corporation of America (later acquired by General Electric), which abandoned the site in 1924.

After a number of interim incarnations, the Evans era began when the federal government acquired the site for electronic research and development. They named it for Lieutenant Colonel Paul W. Evans, a World War I Signal Corps officer. The area was central to the development of radar, an invention that was vital to winning the war and a story that is told with compelling interest here by the Radio Technology Museum of New Jersey. After the war, one could say that Camp Evans scientists "went to the moon" by virtue of the Project Diana experiments that "bounced" signals off this celestial body. An enormous variety of communication and earth-orbiting satellite work that was conducted here, which is beyond the ambit of this brief account, is remembered through a variety of buildings and displays that include on the Diana site the massive TIROS dish antenna, the most visible reminder of an enormously important earth observation satellite program that, among its contributions, led to the accurate forecast of weather.

Camp Evans was threatened after the army closed the base in 1993. The various proposals for its reuse would have destroyed much or all of its scientific past. The Information Age organization undertook a massive preservation and reuse project to save the camp for history, a project more extensive than any precedent in Monmouth County. Its work that embraces reopening once derelict buildings, caring for scientific structures and attracting a consortium of participants has installed a number of museums and remains ongoing at publication. The New Jersey Shipwreck Museum demonstrates why the New Jersey coast is known as the "Graveyard of the Atlantic" through informative displays and recovered artifacts. The National Broadcasting Hall of Fame, housed in Freehold in the 1970s but later relocated out of state, has returned to Monmouth County and is housed here. Their exhibits produce instant nostalgia among those who remember their early listening/viewing appliances and a "You watched that?" reaction of amazement among the younger set. A number of computer and radio exhibits convey how the speed of modern discovery can quickly turn an innovation into an antique.

www.infoage.org; 732.280.3000
Access: 1:00–5:00 p.m. Sundays; events; WOM. Parking: lot.

Historic Village at Allaire (NRHP 1974)
Pine Creek Railroad
Allaire State Park
4265 Atlantic Avenue
Allaire, NJ

The Historic Village at Allaire is a reclaimed, restored industrial village of a former bog iron refining operation, which in the years surrounding 1830

The remains of an industrial settlement await the visitor to Allaire, once known as the Deserted Village, but the ruins of the old furnace may be the most impressive structure in the park.

was an important Monmouth County industry. The adjacent but separately operated Pine Creek Railroad make Allaire a two-stops-in-one state park visit—one that will enthrall the entire family.

An iron forge that processed the area's abundant bog iron is believed to have existed here since the Revolution. Other forges operated in a number of pine barren locales, as they took advantage of the region's abundant resources of not only bog iron but also the timber needed to fire the forge. Following James P. Allaire's purchase of the forge and surrounding land in 1822, he improved the property, replaced many of its buildings and made the place, which he named the Howell Works, a significant industrial operation. However, before long, the bog iron industry was made obsolete after the discovery of rock ore and anthracite coal, along with the hot blast method of production. The Howell Works closed in 1846; James P. Allaire died in 1858. His widow remained with their only child, Hal, who was born at the works in 1847 and stayed alone after his mother's death in 1879. After Hal's death in 1901 and brief interim ownership by W.J. Harrison, famed journalist Arthur Brisbane bought the old village, the works and six thousand acres in 1907. During the 1890s, the former carpenter shop was remodeled into the Allaire Inn, which, in conjunction with its restaurant, did a thriving business early in the new century with an emerging automobile excursion trade. The works became known as the Deserted Village, a nickname that added a cachet of mystery to the place. Brisbane built a mansion across the road from the present park, gave an extensive tract to the Boy Scouts for a camp at one dollar annually for twenty years, eventually lived here year-round and expressed his intent to give the land to the public. Following his death in 1936, his widow, Phoebe, made the first major gift to the State of New Jersey in 1940. Restoration and beating back the ravages of nature began after World War II. An extensive preservation project was required to produce the popular restored village that visitors enjoy in the midst of Allaire State Park.

The village is operated by Allaire Village, Inc., a private nonprofit corporation that undertakes the village's interpretation and produces its programs. Many portray nineteenth-century life to create a "you are there" experience of the heyday of Allaire.

The Pine Creek Railroad was established in 1952, located at a Route 9, Marlboro site. The line, part of the New Jersey Museum of Transportation, was moved to Allaire in 1964 where enthusiastic, hard-working, self-supporting volunteers restore and operate vintage steam and other locomotives on a narrow gauge railroad and offer rides to visitors. Hours are typically weekends in spring and fall and daily in summer. Check site.

Village: www.allairevillage.org; 732.919.3500
Access: extensive hours year-round; events; WOM. Parking: lot.

Railroad: njmt.org; 732.938.5524

Old Wall Historical Society Buildings
Allgor-Barkalow Homestead and Blansingburg School No. 99 (Homestead, NRHP 1984)
1701 New Bedford Road
Wall, NJ 07719

The three buildings operated by the Old Wall Historical Society provide an in-depth look into the rural roots of a now substantially developed township. The interiors of the homestead and school convey the atmosphere of their times.

The Allgor-Barkalow Homestead was built in the early nineteenth century by farmer John W. Allgor, who was succeeded by his son, James L. who, around 1844 opened a general store that he operated for a time in the front of this residence and later in a separate building across the street. James was active in public life, having held long tenures as township committeeman and postmaster while also serving as a shore salvage master. The property passed to his son-in-law, Job S. Barkalow, who had married Allgor's daughter, Lavinia. The house and its outbuildings remained as the seat of a farm until passing into public ownership in 1972. The building, which is interpreted

The Allgor-Barkalow Homestead was likely begun by John W. Allgor in the second quarter of the nineteenth century. It once served as general store, post office and community center.

The Blansingburg Schoolhouse Museum, built in 1855, was relocated here from Sea Girt Avenue and Old Mill Road following donation to the society in 1999.

for the nineteenth century, contains a variety of artifacts and a genealogy research library.

The Blansingburg School, which opened in 1855 as local district 9, but was later County District No. 99 stood on Sea Girt Avenue where it served for educational use until 1936 when it began its second incarnation as a business building. The former school, located on Frank Newman's business property adjacent to his hardware and feed store, was used as a lawnmower repair shop. It was at risk when the Newmans sold the property in 1999 but was rescued by donation to the Township of Wall, which relocated the building to New Bedford Road, undertook repairs in conjunction with the historical society and installed utilities. The refitted building was dedicated for interpretive use on September 23, 2001. Ancient furnishings and wall maps convey in this large single room an authentic atmosphere of bygone school days. How effective is the restoration? As Frances Bruno, an officer of the historical society, told the author, "It looks just as it did when I went here (1927–1936)."

The Morris-Allgor-Kittell wheelwright shop will be the society's third exhibition building following restoration that is ongoing at publication. Located across from their school on the east side of New Bedford Road, the structure is one of the oldest brick buildings in the county. The society traced the shop's documentary trail to the sale of its builder, Jackson Morris, who is believed to have erected the place around 1840, to James L. Allgor, the nearby store owner. The building's long esteem and importance to the township's history is reflected by its selection in 1957 for placement on the municipal seal.

Access: 1:00–4:00 p.m.; WOM. Parking: lot.

West Long Branch

Monmouth University, Murry Guggenheim House (Library)
(NRHP 1978)
Cedar and Norwood Avenues
West Long Branch, NJ 07764

The Murry Guggenheim residence is an outstanding Beaux-Arts house that was completed in 1905 on the site of Normahurst, the seat of publisher Norman L. Munro (1842–1894) who built the surrounding exclusive summer home colony still known as Norwood Park.

Thomas Hastings's commission for the Murry Guggenheim house was the design that won him the Medal of Honor of the New York Chapter of the American Institute of Architects in 1906. It has served as a library for Monmouth University since 1961.

Henrietta, Munro's widow, retained the place for rental after his death, leasing it for the 1899 season to Vice President Garrett Hobart but losing the house in a mysterious fire on March 17, 1902. Carrere and Hastings designed the mansion, which earned them in 1906 (not 1903 as has been repeatedly cited) the gold Medal of Honor of the New York Chapter of the American Institute of Architects. (See also First Presbyterian Church of Rumson, page 71.) Murry was a son of Meyer, the patriarch of the American family that amassed a fortune in copper mining and smelting, although his brother, Solomon, may be better known, as he founded in New York the art museum bearing his name. Murry died in 1939, ten years after he and his wife established the Murry and Leonie Guggenheim Foundation that gave the house to what was then Monmouth College after her death in 1959. The college opened a library there, which was named in their honor. The building has expanded while retaining some of its residential integrity.

www.library.monmouth.edu/about/mansion/cottage; 732.571.3400
Access: liberal open hours. Parking: lot; guest spaces.

Monmouth University, Woodrow Wilson Hall (Shadow Lawn II; Hubert Templeton Parson House) (NRHP 1978)
400 Cedar Avenue (at Norwood Avenue)
West Long Branch, NJ 07764

The histories of the present and the first Shadow Lawn are so often conflated that they are distinguished by designations I and II. The contemporary Woodrow Wilson Hall of Monmouth University, or Shadow Lawn II, is the 1930 Italian Renaissance Hubert Templeton Parson house. Shadow Lawn I was the 1904 John A. McCall house in which Woodrow Wilson spent the later part of 1916 and the locale of his front-porch reelection campaign.

John A. McCall, the president of New York Life Insurance Company, bought a number of farms and then hired Harry G. Creiger to design his huge mansion, one that was essentially an Italian Renaissance Revival house set behind an oversized Neo-Classical portico. He lost his job and house in a scandal that ran rampant through the life insurance industry in the years after he moved in. Following brief tenures by two interim figures, retail magnate Joseph B. Greenhut became the second prominent owner. He held the place at a time when Long Branch business interests

Shadow Lawn II was 1930 replacement of an earlier mansion that was destroyed by fire in 1927. Woodrow Wilson's use of the Shadow Lawn I in 1916 is the inspiration for Monmouth University's name for the building, Wilson Hall.

hatched hopes to revive local commercial and resort activity by attracting another president, as they attempted to replicate the notoriety and attention that earlier chief executives brought to the city. After Shadow Lawn was offered free of charge, Wilson insisted on paying a fair rental; his 1916 stay is history. Parson, the president of F.W. Woolworth, once the nation's premier retailer, bought Shadow Lawn in 1918 but lost it to fire on January 7, 1927.

Country house specialist Horace Trumbauer's Italian Renaissance palace was plagued by well-known delays, change orders and cost overruns, excesses whose details are beyond the scope of this brief account. Hubert appeared to give his wife, Mayzie, an unlimited budget, and she exceeded it. Its standing as the costliest house built in Monmouth County stood for about three quarters of a century, but Parson's fall was faster than the mansion's rise. Shunned by local society at his 1930 opening, he subsequently faced mandatory retirement, loss of his hefty salary, foreclosure and a premature death. Brief interim incarnations preceded the reuse and restoration by Monmouth University.

The house, although adapted for educational function, retains much of its residential character; thus a visit is like a step back into the twilight of the age of splendor. If the interior seems familiar, you may recall it from the film *Annie*, as Shadow Lawn was the set for Daddy Warbucks's mansion. Woodrow Wilson Hall was designated a National Historic Landmark in 1985.

www.monmouth.edu/wilson_hall; 732.571.3400
Access: liberal open hours. Parking: lot; guest spaces.

Old First United Methodist Church
197 Locust Avenue
West Long Branch, NJ 07764

Old First United Methodist Church is important as the first built in Monmouth County for a faith that would assume spiritual and social significance in its nearby shore area.

Methodist worship in the Long Branch area began circa 1780, while the congregation known as Old First United Methodist was organized in 1809. They completed this edifice in 1819. See the fine museum in the lower level of their nearby hall.

Methodist worship in the Long Branch area, which began in the 1780s, centered at the nearby Free Church, begun in 1791. A division in the Methodist community between Methodist Episcopals and the Independent Methodists known as Congerites for their leader Zenas Conger motivated the former group to found this church in 1809, the year its ten-year construction project for this edifice began. A twelve-foot section was added in 1842–43, likely the rear, while a thirteen-foot addition, including the bell tower, was built in 1874. The latter followed shortly after the 1869 establishment of the major Methodist summer meeting place of Ocean Grove. Stained glass was installed in 1903; most are memorials.

The historical museum in the church hall's basement is a hidden treasure that commemorates not only the church's past but also the West Long Branch area. The cemetery that surrounds the church has a number of noteworthy interments. The most significant historical monument honors the memory of the 240 who perished in 1854 aboard the *New Era*, a ship that wrecked off the Monmouth shore carrying immigrants from Bremen, Germany.

www.oldfirstchurch.org; 732.222.4232
Access: worship; events. Parking: lot.

CHAPTER 4

WESTERN REGION

ALLENTOWN

Imlay House
26 South Main Street
Allentown, NJ 08501

The John Imlay house, one of the finest Georgian houses in New Jersey, merits viewing and esteem for that lofty stature. While its adaptive use for retail may inhibit understanding of the interior, the whole is a rewarding experience and a tale of survivorship.

The house, alternately designated "mansion" for look, size and masterful construction in every detail, was built circa 1790 after John Imlay, a prosperous Revolutionary War–era Philadelphia merchant, returned to his native area to retire. Remaining until his 1813 death, John was succeeded here by his son, William, who occupied it until 1880.

In the rear of the large room-size entry hall is a richly detailed staircase that Imlay family tradition claims a master carpenter took six months to build. Landings are unsupported, the balusters are mahogany and a scroll sun ornament is carved under each riser. Rooms are in each corner of the house in the Georgian manner. Eleven of the house's fifteen rooms contain fireplaces, a number of which are surrounded with richly carved mantels. Wallpaper of a special variety made in small squares, which was purchased in London in 1794 and mounted in the parlor, was bought by the Metropolitan

While no longer a residence, the colonial era's grandest house in the region still effuses grandeur as visitors step inside the hall and the several shops that now occupy a commercial building.

Museum of Art in the late 1920s for placement on the walls of the Haverhill Room in its American Wing.

Adaptive use came early, first as Mary Evans Gordon's boardinghouse around the 1920s, then as Dr. Walter Farmer's "hospital," which was dedicated on Sunday June 6, 1937. Farmer was a "character" who was eager to use his surgical specialty and helped terminate unwanted pregnancies before such service was readily available. Most patients were from out of town, as wary locals often went elsewhere. The building was converted to its present retail use at an unspecified date.

Access: commercial retail building. Parking: street.

Allentown Historic District (NRHP 1982)
Along Main Street and some side streets
Allentown, NJ 08501

Allentown's historic district can suggest even to the casual observer both the growth of an old small commercial center for an agrarian region and the perils of later development. The endearing streetscape is characterized by well-preserved vintage buildings, but its fragility is evidenced by heavy motor traffic on ways designed for horse and wagons. The increasing vehicular flow and their constant pounding occasioned the replacement of the Main Street Bridge over Doctors Creek, completed not long before this book's publication.

The four-story former mill is Allentown's most visible building. It is a presence that harkens back to the place's origins when Nathan Allen's substantial 1706 land purchases included 110 acres on Doctors Creek, a tract that embraces the site where he built a gristmill. Its surrounding area became known as Allen's Town. The mill building at 42 South Main Street, a later replacement dating from 1855, earned National Register listing in 1978, years after its milling career ended in the 1960s. The Mill House still stands at number 38.

The variety of commercial and residential buildings that line Main stem from a business center that prospered by drawing clientele from three additional nearby counties, Mercer, Ocean and Burlington. The intersection with Waker Avenue was once home to two former occupancies suggestive of a business center, a hotel on the south side and the Farmers National Bank, the builder of the pie-shaped structure on the north side. Allentown, organized as a borough in 1889, is a tiny municipality of about two thousand residents that is governed from a storefront; its municipal hall is located at 8 North Main. Spiritual life was also centered on Main, but not all of its churches remain. Some required larger quarters and relocated nearby, but the Methodist building is adaptively used as a library.

The visitor can observe the evidence of a built environment that reflects the march of time: as one moves away from the main intersection, the buildings are typically larger, while some are set back from the street as they become progressively younger. Compact Allentown is best seen on foot, a means where no vehicle will stand in the way of absorbing the centuries of history that rise from the sidewalks.

Business association site www.AllentownNJ.com
Access: public streets. Parking: street.

ENGLISHTOWN

Village Inn (NRHP 1972)
2 Water Street
Englishtown, NJ 07726

The Village Inn that has long been celebrated for its claimed role at the time of the Battle of Monmouth still stands through the exertions of the Battleground Historical Society. They saved the place when in 1978 it was threatened with destruction following the death of the last tavern owner,

The colonial-era Village Inn is interpreted as an eighteenth-century tavern that reflects its notoriety at the time of the Battle of Monmouth when combating forces used the inn.

Hazel Fleming Applegate. The society's work has revealed much of the building's history, removed some later additions and resulted in the Village Inn's present role as a restored colonial tavern.

The building's oldest section, the three bays on the west, or left as one faces the building, was initially two rooms in one and a half stories, perhaps built in the second quarter of the eighteenth century and apparently initially occupied as a tailor shop. It was later expanded to two and a half stories, to which the two bays on the east were added, perhaps around 1815. Viewers familiar with long-extant historical imagery of the Village Inn may note that other additions on the west and a center gable were removed. Its incarnation as a tavern, which likely began in the third quarter of the eighteenth century, has been traced through the documentary trail of innkeeper Moses Davis, the namesake of the place that during the past century became known as the Davis Inn. A surviving account book of the inn proved that it was patronized by a number of colonial militiamen, but the building's notoriety has been for the claim of its use by General George Washington, notably for the court-martial of General Charles Lee for his conduct at the Battle of Monmouth. The history of the Village Inn has come into question in recent years. While it has been claimed that the Village Inn was the site of these events, Battleground Historical Society officers at the time of publication believe concrete evidence is needed to confirm that the Village Inn and not the other tavern in town was the actual site.

The prominent corner lot was sought for commercial purposes prior to the inn's rescue by the Battleground Historical Society, which undertook architectural and archeological studies that revealed the building's significance and provided evidence to guide the restoration. The project was aided by a substantial commitment of federal Community Development Block Grant Program financing, as well as funds raised by the society. What remains retains the flavor and feeling of an old tavern. In addition, photograph exhibitions at the inn portray the region's evolution.

www.thevillageinn.org; 732.536.3351
Access: events; by appointment; WOM. Parking: municipal lot across Main Street opposite inn.

FREEHOLD BOROUGH

Battle Monument and Monument Park
71 Court Street
Freehold, NJ 07728

The Battle Monument is the most visible symbol of the critical Revolutionary conflict that is described in the entry for the Monmouth Battlefield State Park (page 147). Its construction, completed with major public and private support that was attained at a time prior to the regular erection of monumental symbols, was a major accomplishment by its local backers.

The earliest calls for an appropriate memorial began around 1850 when a few aged veterans of the Revolution were still alive. However, these and repeated revivals of the campaign that were made over the decades failed, causing perceptive observers to believe that if nothing was accomplished by the battle's centennial, a memorial would likely never be built. Freehold resident and former governor Joel Parker and local newspaper editor James S. Yard were the driving forces that organized the Monmouth Battle Monument Association, which raised funds privately and spurred significant contributions from the State of New Jersey and federal governments. The family of Daniel S. Schanck donated the triangular plot that became Monument Park.

While the tall shaft and statue dominate the Monument Park landscape, make certain to see the monument close up to view the five bas-reliefs by noted sculptor James Edward Kelly that were the artistic highlights of the project.

An architectural competition for the monument's design, notably its well-laid-out base, was won by Emelin T. Littell and Douglas Smythe. Its cornerstone was laid on the June 28, 1878 centennial anniversary of the battle, accompanied by considerable local rejoicing and fanfare. However, the event, although a major milestone, was a celebratory pause in the major fundraising required for completion. In addition, important artistic decisions were yet to be made. James Edward Kelly was selected to design five Revolutionary scenes to be executed in bronze bas-relief plaques and also other, smaller plaques that portrayed the seals of the original thirteen states. The statue of *Columbia Triumphant*, which was obtained from a Quincy, Massachusetts stone yard, was for practical purposes an artistic afterthought, as it was hardly mentioned while the builders focused on the bronzes. The figure now atop the monument is a replica, placed there after the original was struck by lightning in 1894 and damaged beyond repair. Its origin, which remained obscure for over a century, was revealed only when Columbia Triumphant Park was established; it is described in the next entry.

The bas-reliefs merit close inspection. These sculptural representations of *Ramsey Defending His Gun*, *Washington Rallying the Troops*, *Molly Pitcher*, *Council of War at Hopewell* and *Wayne's Charge* are early works of the artist who enjoyed a long career that included a number of public commissions. After death, his reputation faded into obscurity, but his popularity has been resurrected in recent years after discovery of his large body of work on Civil War figures. The lengthy project and eager public anticipation culminated with a major dedication celebration on November 13, 1884.

The grounds were given over to the State of New Jersey at a time when counties did not maintain parks; they were transferred to the County of Monmouth in 1999. While the park became a place of public veneration and is still used at times for large gatherings, the Battle Monument is too often regarded as a directional landmark, perhaps for entering the courthouse or downtown, but it demands a closer look. Street parking is ample, while an interpretive plaque mounted on the well-traveled Court Street should draw in the passerby via its account of significance.

Access: public park. Parking: west side of Court Street.

Columbia Triumphant
5 East Main Street
Freehold, NJ 07728

The bust of the Battle Monument's statue was shipped to a stone yard in Quincy, Massachusetts, to serve as a model for a replica because the original model was no longer usable. After the replica was completed, the monument association sought the bust's return to ensure that it could not be used as a model for another monument. After its return to Freehold, the bust was not retained by the county but was literally cast aside where it fell to a dismal fate as a decoration in a nearby stone yard. It stood along the local railroad tracks where it wound up as a target for bottle throwers, as it sank amid accumulating garbage. Since the old figure lacked local interest or claim, *Columbia Triumphant* was spirited out of town by a would-be rescuer who mounted it in his junk yard but treated it as a subject of respect and honor. It was literally forgotten for decades until the possibility of its return was

This bust was returned to Quincy, Massachusetts, to serve as a model for the replica now on the monument, was sent back to Freehold after the replica was made, was removed from town for a long spell, then was finally returned to her own small plot and individual honor.

brought to the attention of the County by local historian Carl N. Steinberg. The statue would come with a price and, after being duly ransomed, largely through a fundraising campaign spearheaded by Steinberg, would wait a long spell for the plan, design and construction of a new Main Street home adjacent to the Hall of Records.

The planning process brought focus on the figure's dual historical identity. Both the names *Columbia Triumphant* and *Liberty Triumphant* were used simultaneously around the statue's 1886 installation, which was the year concurrent with the dedication of *Liberty Enlightening the World* in New York Harbor, the event that propelled *Liberty* to assume the mantle of the allegorical female representation of the nation. *Liberty* succeeded *Columbia*, which had followed an earlier female known as *America*. A key, visible characteristic of *Columbia* was her tiara of stars, which made the Freehold figure decidedly *Columbia*. After a long lapse for a short space, Columbia Triumphant Park was dedicated on June 27, 2003. The small park, fitted with benches and decorated with plants, was laid out between the sidewalk and a parking lot adjacent to the Hall of Records Annex. The statue's nose, broken at an unknown time in its difficult life, is left unrepaired, as the break is considered part of the bust's history.

The figure's exact origin has not been definitively pinpointed, but an excellent inference was offered by art history professor Dr. William Gerdts's estimation that its design based on stylistic appearance was likely dated from the late 1830s or 1840s, the time of the ascendency of *Columbia*. This age may explain why the original yard model that served in 1884 was no longer usable a decade later. It stands to reason that one or more other statues modeled on this figure were earlier carved in what was the granite capital of the east, but the author, who continues his ardent examination of monument statue photographs, has not discovered one.

Access: public park. Parking: street; adjacent lot accessed via Lafayette Street.

Court Street School (NRHP 1995)
140 Court Street
Freehold, NJ 07728

The Court Street School, erected as one of the last segregated schools in New Jersey, is a landmark in the struggle against segregation. It was closed when the New Jersey Constitution of 1947 banned segregation and remained closed in face of parents who resisted sending their white children to the formerly all-black school. The Court Street School reopened only when a steep rise in enrollment compelled its use. In time, triumph over these obstacles earned the school stature as a symbol of America's struggle for equality.

The school, built in 1912 when the future borough was still a town organized within Freehold Township, was designed in the Colonial Revival style by noted Freehold architect Warren H. Conover; he also designed its expansion in 1927. For two generations, the student body was exclusively African American, as de facto segregation was the accepted norm in much of New Jersey. Students were guided by role models such as Principal George I. Reed, who told students, as Lillie Hendry recalled, that he wanted Court

The Court Street School's distinction as the region's last segregated school to be built earned its listing on the National Register of Historic Places.

Street School students to be recognizable "because of the way you behave, because of what you achieve and because of the way you plan for your future."

The aforementioned constitutional ban prompted the borough's school board to draw neighborhood district lines in early 1948, a change that was intended to integrate the Court Street School. However, the refusal of white parents to send their children here prompted the board to close the school for the September 1948 year. The district board, which made a number of unsuccessful attempts to dispose of the building, first met here in December 1952, perhaps to demonstrate that they still owned the property. Finally, desperate for classroom space during the post–World War II baby boom, the Court Street building reopened in September 1953 as an integrated school. White resistance was expressed in frustration by a board member who stated at their September 21, 1953 meeting, "The situation is that Hudson Street has too many and Court Street has the least and the pupil load would be evenly divided if parents living in a zone send their children where they are supposed to."

After local instruction ended, reportedly in 1974, the building was given an administrative function and sold to the County of Monmouth in 1981.

In time after county office use, building occupancy was given to the Court Street School Community Education Center.

www.courtstreetschool.com; 732.303.8724.
Access: events. Parking: lot.

Covenhoven House (NRHP 1974)
150 West Main Street
Freehold, NJ 07728

Covenhoven, one of the most important houses in Monmouth County, continues to retain notoriety for its use as a headquarters by General Sir Henry Clinton prior to the Battle of Monmouth. Its significance, however, began at construction when a wealthy Dutch farmer built a large house that architecturally reflected the emergence of the Georgian style and the blending of Dutch culture into the prevailing English. A fine state of

This substantial residence has multiple names in historical references, including General Clinton's Headquarters, the Moreau House and the Hankinson House for later owners, but it is now known as the Covenhoven House for the building of what is arguably the county's most important mid-eighteenth-century house.

preservation, distinctive interior finishing and informative interpretive programs of the Monmouth County Historical Association make Covenhoven a compelling visit.

William A. Covenhoven and his wife, Elizabeth Van Cleaf, each of whom inherited significant sums of money, sought to show their new wealth by the acquisition of land and the construction of an impressive house. After his circa 1750 purchase of 180 acres west of the village, Covenhoven soon afterward hired John Davies to build one of the largest and most pretentious houses in the area. The association of Davies with this house was determined through architectural detective work. Key evidence was the knowledge that Davies had built Old Tennent Church (page 150) in 1751–52. Comparison of it and Covenhoven show distinct construction similarities that reflect the work of a skilled, in fact the same, master craftsman. Davies's touch was also discovered at the Matawan Burrowes Mansion (page 26), a revelation that helped date that house.

The Covenhovens' melding into English culture is bolstered by their spiritual affiliation. Although baptized in the Dutch Reformed Church, they joined the Presbyterian Church at Tennent and were among the largest donors to their building fund. Covenhoven incorporated some Dutch elements in their Georgian dwelling. Among the house's outstanding interior appointments are finely detailed paneling on all major fireplace walls, cupboards with glazed doors, carved shell bonnets and painted woodwork decoration in the master bedroom. The house's long reference as Freehold's outstanding residence has brought it numerous names in historical literature, notably General Clinton's headquarters but also the Hankinson and the Moreau House for significant later owners. The identification with Covenhoven made over the past few decades reflects the custom of naming for the original builder. The cultural background of the Covenhoven history is only briefly outlined here; Joseph Hammond's research paper "The Covenhoven House: A Study In Cultural Transition," produced for and located at the Monmouth County Historical Association, merits careful study by the interested visitor.

www.monmouthhistory.org
Access: Thursday–Saturday, 1:00–4:00 p.m., May–September; WOM. Parking: lot.

Main Street Streetscape
East (of Hall of Records) and West Main Street
Freehold, NJ 07728

Freehold's Main Street has the characteristic look of a once rural county seat, a collection of public, residential and institutional buildings that suggest stature as a former busy center of commerce and current seat of government. Indeed, in recent decades, government has expanded as business has shrunk. A knowing viewer can absorb much through casual observation.

For an ancient town, Freehold has relatively few buildings that date prior to 1850 because Freehold built new ones during its expansive, prosperous stage. Downtown Main's oldest are the Greek Revival structures at 42 and 49 East Main. The attractive 1904 Carnegie Library at 28½ East Main is a reminder that public buildings were usually erected in the heart of a town when most of the populous walked. A conflagration on October 29, 1873, destroyed the block on the north side, west of Court Street, so as a consequence, most of that street was rebuilt at the same time. Many buildings retain the appealing look of their Commercial Italianate style, notably 3 West Main which has an attractive cornice crest not unlike the one on the Brown Building nearby at 16 East Main. The remodeling of some on this block, however, belie their age, including the ineffective changes to 1 West Main Street on the corner of Court Street and the handsome Neo-Classical façade placed on 19 West Main in 1924. On the south side, the 1895 Perrine Building at 12–16 commands attention by its three gables and size, which gave rise to its old nickname of the Big Red Store. Crossing Throckmorton Street are the tracks of the ancient Freehold and Jamesburg Agricultural Railroad (later the Pennsylvania), Monmouth's first rail line. Passenger service ended in 1962, while the 1895 station has been converted to other use.

Main's western stem is dotted with fine houses, some of which have been converted to commercial use and appealing churches. The largest edifice is the First Presbyterian at 118 West Main, while the largest congregation is a block south of Main at 16 McLean Street, the fine Gothic Revival St. Rose of Lima. Its locale is a reminder of nineteenth-century bias that barred the Catholics from Main Street. The First Baptist Church at 81 West Main also possesses architectural distinction. Residential stylistic variety from the Greek Revival through the various styles utilized throughout the Victorian era, plus a few Colonial Revivals near Park Avenue enable the stroller to perceive the progressive development of these blocks through changing architecture. Of particular interest is an architect's own house, as 2 Yard Street at the northwest corner of West Main, was the aforementioned Warren H. Conover's residence.

Access: public streets. Parking: street and public lots on Lafayette Street and Market Yard, south of Main and east of South Street.

Monmouth County Hall of Records (former Courthouse)
1 East Main Street
Freehold, NJ 07728

This centrally located area was chosen for Monmouth's first permanent courthouse, and when completed in 1715, the future Freehold became known as Monmouth Courthouse and was established as the county seat, making this spot the core of Monmouth public life for four centuries.

No image exists of this insubstantial building destroyed by fire in December 1727, which was followed by a second court in 1731. While this building was central to county activity in the Revolution and became an iconic image through a Carrie Swift painting, it deteriorated markedly and was repaired in 1791 to extend its utility for another fifteen years. But it

The contemporary view is a 1931 remodeling of an 1874 courthouse built around three surviving walls of an earlier structure that burned in 1873. However, the remodeled building has gained historic stature in its own right.

was later replaced by a more substantial, handsome Neo-Classical stone and brick edifice that measured sixty feet across and forty feet deep. It stood adjacent to a separate 1803 county clerk's building that was on the edge of Court Street, which stood until its replacement in 1851. A major fire in the court in 1855 was followed by the addition of a second story to the adjacent clerk's building, which was subsequently connected to the court, changes that led to the building that is on the site today.

The reconstituted court and county clerk's building were substantially destroyed by fire during the October 30, 1873 conflagration that leveled the block to the west, although it is believed that three walls survived, with the present building reconstructed around them to a Neo-Classical design by Austin Patterson, an architect-builder who was also Freeholder Director. The fast-track project was ready for its first trial on April 18, 1874.

There have been many changes to the building in the intervening near century and a half, including both additions and removals. Notable was a jail and jailer's residence, once a separate structure, which had been added to the building on its northeast in 1875 and subsequently removed, the former following the 1970 opening of the present jail. Significant additions were made in 1884, 1903 and 1916. The many changes account for one-time former exterior walls that are now hidden inside the building and interior offices and halls that are not on the same level. The building's present handsome appearance followed a major 1931 expansion and remodeling designed by Leon Cubberley. Following the opening of the present courthouse in 1955, the character and major occupancy of the old court changed, and it was renamed the Monmouth County Hall of Records. It remains the seat of county government. The hall is linked on the east to the interior of a former theater that survived a devastating fire on April 7, 1962, a sympathetic extension in which this annex appears part of the original building.

Access: county business. Parking: street; adjacent lot.

Monmouth County Historical Association Museum and Library
70 Court Street
Freehold, NJ 07728

The Monmouth County Historical Association has earned superlatives here for collections of art, artifacts, decorative arts, education and exhibitions, along with the depth and breadth of the documentary and in-print holdings

This 1931 museum designed to appear as a Georgian-era building houses an outstanding collection of art, decorative arts, a wide variety of artifacts and memorabilia as well as a reference library rich in county history.

of its library. The facility is simply the heart and soul of the history of Monmouth County and a "must see" in order to obtain an in-depth insight into the county's history.

The organization was founded in 1897 by wealthy residents of the Middletown–Red Bank–Shrewsbury area, many of them summer dwellers who were led and inspired by Catherine Gallup Reed, a New York educator who owned a family compound bordering the north bank of the Navesink River near the Oceanic Bridge in Middletown Township. The association had no headquarters in its early decades, although active founders preserved history through study, lectures and articles, along with the collecting of documents. They were close to building a museum in Red Bank around 1920, but the planned facility at Harding Road and Branch Avenue did not materialize. The association's attention was drawn to the county seat in view of the proximity of official records in Freehold. After they rejected a proposal to buy the Main Street home of former governor Joel Parker, David Vanderveer Perrine donated the Court Street lot. J. Hallam Conover was hired to design the Neo-Georgian building that was erected at the height of the Colonial Revival. Conover (1897–1972) was then in practice with his father, Warren H. Conover. The firm specialized in the Colonial Revival, which they employed in many commissions at Freehold and elsewhere, as the town's important role in the formative years of the nation endeared the colonial imagery to the local populace. The October 1931 opening of the building inspired numerous gifts, the makings of a superb collection that has enjoyed enormous growth, holdings that are particularly rich in decorative arts and paintings.

The association's research library is deep in manuscripts and genealogical resources, along with the usual printed books, maps and ephemeral material.

www.monmouthhistory.org; 732.462.1466
Access: museum, Tuesday–Saturday, 10:00 a.m.–4:00 p.m.; library, Wednesday–Saturday, 10:00 a.m.–4:00 p.m.; events; WOM. Parking: street, west side; watch time limit restriction.

St. Peter's Church (NRHP 1998)
33 Throckmorton Street
Freehold, NJ 07728

While the original design is attributed to the distinguished colonial-era architect Robert Smith, the church today reflects nineteenth-century Gothic Revival alterations.

St. Peter's is the oldest building in Freehold and a witness to the American Revolution. The congregation, which dates its origin to 1702, was first located at Topanemus, near today's Marlboro, prior to receiving a charter from King George II in 1736.

The church purchased their Freehold lot as early as 1738, but knowledge of the origin of the present building is obscure. It may date from the 1771 proposal to build a new church at Monmouth Courthouse, as the village of Freehold was then called, a structure that remained unfinished for years. The building is believed to have sheltered wounded during and after the Battle of Monmouth. St. Peter's was originally a simple rectangular plan Georgian building. The present church reflects Gothic Revival alterations made, perhaps, in the third quarter of the nineteenth century.

Adjacent on the north, the Greek Revival rectory, believed to have been started circa 1820–40, was expanded and altered later in the nineteenth century. The parish house on the south, near Main Street, was built in 1924 and remodeled in 1964. The few gravestones near the corner were moved from the church's ancient cemetery at Topanemus.

www.stpetersfreehold.org; 732.431.8383
Access: worship; events. Parking: street.

FREEHOLD TOWNSHIP

Jewish Heritage Museum of Monmouth County
310 Mounts Corner Drive
Freehold, NJ 07728

The museum, which sits near the northwest corner of Mounts Corner shopping center, was established as a consequence of township regulators exacting an agreement whereby the center's owner gave a ninety-nine-year lease for historical purposes as a remedy for zoning issues. The structure's first incarnation as a barn is readily detectable, but the retail space at grade may not suggest that a museum is located within. However, the museum's finely restored second-story quarters convey the atmosphere of a barn in modernized space.

According to its website,

> The Jewish Heritage Museum of Monmouth County is dedicated to the promotion of public awareness of the County's Jewish heritage for the

Retail at grade may disguise the existence of a museum and cultural center upstairs where retained interior building elements convey the structure's past as a barn.

education and enjoyment of both children and adults. Its mission is to present exhibits, programs and publications that celebrate, explore and illustrate the rich and unique history of the Jewish residents of Monmouth County, N.J. and their contribution to the community.

Its occupancy of the entire second floor includes performance space to reflect a museum heritage mission that embraces the arts.

The museum's most fascinating artifact stems from the building's agricultural past. It is a large water tank that rests on heavy beams positioned about ten feet over the floor. The six-foot-tall and six-foot-diameter wood tank has a capacity of 1,300 gallons; the contents alone would weigh over five tons. The means for collection or filling are not known, but its downspout suggests the tank supplied the housed animals.

www.jhmomc.org; 732.252.6990
Access: Tuesday, 10:00 a.m.–3:00 p.m.; Thursday, 10:00 a.m.–3:00 p.m. and 6:00–9:00 p.m.; Sunday, 11:00 a.m.–3:00 p.m.; events; WOM. Parking: shopping center lot.

Oakley Farm House (NRHP 1990)
(Freehold Township Historic Preservation Commission)
189 Oakley Drive
Freehold, NJ 07728

The Walker Combs Hartshorne Farmstead, commonly known as the Oakley Farm for its last owners, reflects three centuries of a once rural township's agrarian roots. The site of the regularly expanded house amid outbuildings conveys an image of a working farm. The origins appear to be an eight-by-ten-foot cabin built at an unknown date, conceivably in the first quarter of the eighteenth century; its earliest expansion was made at an unknown date. The first of the namesake owners, George Walker, bought the land in 1720; in 1801, his descendants sold to Elijah Combs, who farmed 240 acres and likely gave the house its present appearance. The Hartshornes were descendants of Richard, who was among Monmouth's earliest settlers and is a major seventeenth-century figure in Middletown. A branch of the family later settled in Freehold. The first of the family here, Richard S. Hartshorne Sr., who bought the place in 1842, was succeeded in 1873 by his son, Acton, an important member of the Monmouth bar who in time leased the farm

From likely early eighteenth-century origins as a small cabin, the Oakley Farm House has grown through a number of additions, the last in 1924, which give the place its present shape.

and then sold it to Charles Oakley Jr. in 1911. The Township of Freehold bought a by then reduced 6-acre property from an Oakley in 1997.

While the Oakley Farm House has a fascinating chain of title, its appeal to the visitor is the simplicity of the large house set among surviving outbuildings.

www.ftheritage.org; 732.577.9766
Access: house, the third Sunday of June through September, by appointment; WOM; grounds, year-round during daylight. Parking: on site and Oakley Drive.

West Freehold School Museum
(Freehold Township Historic Preservation Commission)
209 Wemrock Road
Freehold, NJ 07728

The West Freehold School is an infrequent reminder that the West Freehold area was a village, one that has been nearly effaced. The nearby modern development makes the old crossroads resemble a highway. An interpretive program of the Freehold Township Preservation Commission enables the visitor to step back to a nineteenth-century educational environment.

Franklin Ellis's 1885 *History of Monmouth County* suggests a school existed in West Freehold as early as 1818. Other sources report that this lot was

After rural Freehold Township consolidated its numerous small schools in 1936, the municipality closed this and similar one-room examples.

offered for a school in 1842 and that this building was erected in 1847, a time when it was known as the West Freehold Seminary and Collegiate Institute. One wonders if it was a private school, as widespread public education was not prevalent until the third quarter of the nineteenth century. This building served for instructional use until 1935 when township schools were consolidated. The commission has opened a second one-room school, the Georgia School at Georgia and Jackson Mills Roads.

www.ftheritage.org; 732.577.9766
Access: by appointment; WOM. Parking: lot in rear of building.

MANALAPAN

Monmouth Battlefield State Park (Historic District NRHP 1966)
16 Business Route 33
Manalapan, NJ 07726

The June 28, 1778 Battle of Monmouth, one of the war's largest and longest battles, was a watershed event of the Revolution. It effectively ended the formal fighting for the armies in New Jersey and marked a change of the

History painter Emanuel Leutze's *Washington at Monmouth* is the best known artistic symbol of that conflict. It pictures the general rallying the troops of Charles Lee who had ordered a retreat contrary to Washington's order. The artist is also known for his *Washington Crossing the Delaware*.

war's character to a four-year guerilla-type conflict, while its outcome gained newfound respect for the Continental forces, a factor that weighed in future British planning. The 1,818-acre State of New Jersey park commemorates and interprets that battle.

General Sir Henry Clinton led a strategic withdrawal of British forces from Philadelphia in order to consolidate at New York City. He planned a march across New Jersey, one that General George Washington aimed to interrupt with a fight. His light infantry detachment initiated a limited attack on the nineteen-thousand-man British force but was beaten back toward the main army. As a consequence of the major artillery duel that then ensued, British guns were forced to withdraw, and an infantry battle followed. As clashing forces continued into the evening, Washington planned to continue the fighting the next day. However, Clinton, cognizant that his goal was to move his substantial fighting force, a large number of camp followers and an enormous baggage train to New York, withdrew during the night. They marched to the hills of Middletown, where they encamped until able to sail from Loyalist-held Sandy Hook to New York. The action on the field was essentially a draw, but the battle was considered a political victory for Washington who demonstrated that he and the Continentals could hold their own on a battlefield against the British. On the other hand, the praise Clinton merits for the successful movement with minimal loss of an enormous force and its equipment is rarely but not unexpectedly given since the winner of the Revolution writes its history.

The park's second historical role of training camp during the Civil War stemmed, in part, from the presence of Monmouth County's first railroad. This line, little used today, is significant to the history of the park, as it brought nineteenth-century visitors here at a time well prior to the automotive age and the regular touring of historic sites. Rebuilding that line has been proposed for a needed expansion of regional rail commuting facilities. Some, including the author, believe that this is the best choice for a variety of reasons. Others believe that daily rail activity will mar the quiet calm that prevails over this pristine tract, but proponents cite the rail line as now part of the park's history.

The park's visitor's center contains interpretive exhibits and sponsors programs, although the center is scheduled to be closed for reconstruction from late 2011 into early 2013. While there, take note of other buildings present at the battle—some of which may be accessible—and the statue of General von Steuben. Another significant aspect of the area's appeal is the extensive network of walking trails that permit visitors to envision the county's former rural, agrarian state. The 1961 National Historic Landmark designation for the battlefield actually preceded the National Register entry. A nearby Revolutionary tour can be made by visiting sites included in this chapter including Old Tennent Church, also in Manalapan; the Village Inn in Englishtown; the Covenhoven House, which Clinton used as a headquarters, in Freehold; and the Battle Monument, also in Freehold. The Monmouth County Historical Association, opposite the monument on Court Street, has a permanent exhibit on the battle. Farther afield, the civil war nature of the Revolution is represented in Middletown by the homes of slain Patriot Joseph Murray in Poricy Park (page 47) and ardent Loyalist Joseph Taylor at Marlpit Hall (page 42). The British withdrawal routes are marked in Middletown with roadside plaques, as is their encampment site in the hills over Sandy Hook. Matawan's Burrowes Mansion (page 26) was the site of a noteworthy raid.

www.monmouthbattlefield.nj.gov; 732.462.9616
Access: park, daily; visitors center, most days as hours vary with season. Parking: lot.

Old Tennent Church
450 Tennent Road
Tennent, NJ 07763

The Old Tennent Church congregation began around 1692 at a small log church on a one-acre plot at a site known as Free Hill about five miles distant in today's Marlboro Township. This group of Scotch Presbyterians, which dates its formal organization as 1706, first erected a church at the location in Manalapan known as White Hill in 1731. They soon outgrew it and built the present edifice in 1751. The interior of the Georgian-design church is particularly appealing, notably for its raised preacher's pulpit in the center of the chancel and the box pews throughout.

The church's namesake is the Reverend William Tennent Jr., whose service to the congregation spanned the forty-three years prior to his death in 1777. The Battle of Monmouth was fought near the church, which was hit by cannon fragments. Wounded Continentals were cared for inside the church, where some died. Many of the battle's dead are

While Old Tennent Church is well known for its role in the Battle of Monmouth, the box-pews and the raised preacher's platform make an interior visit a must. The cemetery includes graves from soldiers on both sides of that conflict.

buried in the surrounding cemetery, including Lieutenant Colonel Henry Monckton of the British Grenadiers, the highest-ranking officer killed at Monmouth.

The ancient cemetery is famed notably for the aforementioned Revolutionary War interments. In addition, a number of individuals significant to Monmouth County history and a variety of stones and monuments make the cemetery a historic site in its own right. While the older sections are regarded as the more historical, one modern monument along the fence has a great artistic appeal. It is the headstone that contains a bronze sculpture by noted figurative sculptor Donald De Lue. A visit is merited to another graveyard owned by Old Tennent, the Old Scots Burying Ground, located five miles distant on Gordons Corner Road in Marlboro at the site of the congregation's founding. The latter cemetery was entered on the National Register of Historic Places in 2001.

www.oldtennentchurch.org; 732.446.6299
Access: worship; WOM. Parking: lot; cemetery trails but not trail leading to the church.

MARLBORO

Old Brick Reformed Church
490 County Route 520
Marlboro, NJ 07762

The 1826 Old Brick Reformed Church is a fine well-preserved Gothic Revival design in which characteristic pointed arch windows and doors are placed on a simple, front-gabled rectangular plan. Old Brick is likely the first church in Monmouth County designed in this style that became prevalent among Roman Catholic and Protestant Episcopal congregations in the second half of the twentieth century. Its siting amid its old cemetery (where the earliest interments date from the 1740s) and location on an active county highway give the church high visual recognition.

The oldest Reformed congregation in Monmouth County, Old Brick was founded in 1699 as the Reformed Church of the Navesink and was later known as the Dutch Reformed Church of Freehold and Middletown. The congregation also had a church in Holmdel (in what was then Middletown),

This edifice of the Old Brick Reformed Church, which was built in 1826, replaced an earlier one built here in 1732. The earliest interments in the cemetery date from the 1740s.

while the present edifice is the third in the Marlboro area. That 1699 date of origin marks the onset of local preaching by clergy visiting from Brooklyn, from which formal organization followed in 1709. The present simple interior has a raised pulpit under a modern pipe organ and pews in a balcony.

732.946.8860
Access: worship. Parking: lot.

ROOSEVELT

Roosevelt Historic District (NRHP 1983)
Entire Borough
Roosevelt, NJ 08555

Roosevelt was founded as a Depression-era resettlement project of the Works Progress Administration, one planned to serve a Jewish needle worker constituency from New York. Founded as Jersey Homesteads, the town is one of several such projects nationwide but the only one in the region. Period architecture and a population with strong links to its origins gave the community its distinctive social and physical character that resulted in the entire municipality's designation as a National Register historic district.

Roosevelt was conceived as a cooperative agricultural and industrial community for garment workers made unemployed by the Depression. Its origins stemmed from a federal grant in 1933, followed by the establishment of the Jersey Homesteads Corporation to oversee the settlement. Construction began in 1934, while the first families arrived in 1936. The local community was inspired by founder Benjamin Brown, an immigrant from Russia who was experienced with comparable Jewish agricultural cooperatives in the West. The houses were a simple Bauhaus design by architect Alfred Kastner, built as either standalones or semidetached, the latter separated by garages. Many of these boxlike, flat-roof structures remain instantly recognizable. The planned commercial

The Jonathan Sahn sculptured head of Franklin D. Roosevelt is an artistic embodiment of the borough that was renamed for the president after his death in 1945.

activity was a worker-owned and -operated cooperative garment factory, which opened in 1936. A consistent money loser, the failed cooperative ceased operation after four years; a private millinery manufacturer later took over. Cooperative agricultural ventures, which included poultry, dairy and crop operations, also failed.

In 1937, Jersey Homesteads separated from surrounding Millstone Township, and its slightly less than two square miles was incorporated as a borough. Public facilities include a single store, a synagogue, a post office that also opened in 1936 and an elementary school. Roosevelt is a rare town where the only house of worship is a synagogue. While the post office does not deliver, residents picking up mail have made the office a de facto social center. The school was, for practical purposes, a fulcrum for building Roosevelt's artistic and cultural character. The renowned Louis Kahn, then employed by Kastner, had a major hand in the design, but the place is best known for the large mural painted by the famed social realist Ben Shahn, assisted by his wife, Bernarda. Shahn, who did not initially intend to stay in Roosevelt, liked its intellectual-social climate, which prompted him to remain for the rest of his life. His presence and influence attracted numerous other artists who established Roosevelt's enduring cultural traditions.

The federal government, which ended financial support in 1945, sold its houses to the settlers. The borough renamed itself in honor of the president after his death that year. Franklin D. Roosevelt is honored by a large sculptured head by Jonathan Shahn, Ben's son, which stands in an amphitheater that adjoins the school and serves as a space for community events. While under pressure of contemporary issues, including the modification, typically through expansion, of its characteristic but small houses, Roosevelt maintains its distinctive flavor. It remains a fine example of combining elements of the town's original plan—a residential core, together with its factory and community buildings surrounded by park land—and a green belt of farms and woods that provide Roosevelt a buffer from nearby communities.

www.web2sons.org (a comprehensive but unofficial site); 609.448.0539
Access: public streets. Parking: street.

UPPER FREEHOLD

Old Yellow Meeting House (NRHP 1975)
70 Yellow Meeting House Road
Upper Freehold Township, NJ

The Old Yellow Meeting House, the oldest house of worship structure in Monmouth County, which is set on the edge of a sizable cemetery lot, reflects and instills a spirit of history even through a walk on its grounds. The ambiance merits a visit, even regular access to the building.

Tradition states Baptist worship on the site began in 1720, while the present building was erected around 1737 after a converted farmhouse was destroyed by fire. The locals, having been released from association with the mother Baptist church in Middletown, were organized as a separate church in 1766 known as the Crosswicks Baptist Church, an

The Old Yellow Meeting House is the oldest church structure in the County. Maintained as a historic building, it is rarely open for services.

identity retained for seven years prior to renaming as the Upper Freehold Baptist Church. An adjoining parsonage is believed to have been begun at the same time with the construction of the center section, to which additions were made in the early nineteenth century. Itinerant clergy are believed to have served the church in its early years prior to David Jones becoming the first resident minister in 1766. He served until 1775, becoming known in the Continental army during the Revolution as the "Fighting Parson."

Three nearby Baptist churches are outgrowths of this congregation: Jacobstown in 1785, Bordentown in 1821 and Freehold in 1834. Township worship tended to locate in emerging villages, and after the Baptists built a church in 1855 in the Imlaystown section in 1855, this one fell into disuse. However, the cemetery remained active and historically is the most often cited part of the complex. It contains about sixty eighteenth-century headstones, including one belonging to the Reverend John Cowell (died 1760), minister at the time of construction, and represents three centuries of funerary practice.

The abandoned, deteriorated edifice was rescued from destruction by the Friends of the Old Yellow Meeting House, a nonprofit corporation organized in 1975 to save the building. Its estimable results have preserved a building with a simple interior that during its limited use readily reminds the visitor of an ancient house of worship. Events include a summer reunion on the last Sunday of July and a Thanksgiving Eve prayer service.

The Friends of the Old Yellow Meeting House can be reached at PO Box 1737, Imlaystown, NJ 08526. Some information about OYMH may be available on the website of the Upper Freehold Baptist Church at www.upperfreeholdbaptist.org.

Access: church, infrequent events; cemetery, sunrise to sunset. Parking: lot.

Historic Walnford (NRHP 1976)
78 Walnford Road
Upper Freehold Township, NJ

Walnford, the 36-acre remains of an ancient industrial village located in the 1,100-acre Crosswicks Creek Park, is interpreted today to reflect over two hundred years of its evolving history. It is set in a locale with an ages-old atmosphere that reflects serenity unlike any other place in Monmouth County. The reader must visit this site.

Richard Waln, a Philadelphia Quaker who bought the core 180 acres of an established industrial village in 1772, utilized his acquisition as both county estate and business operation. Its stream, Crosswicks Creek, was then a major waterway that provided an outlet to the Delaware River for the production of his farms and mills. Waln's wealth is still reflected on site by his surviving 1773 house, which was the largest colonial-era residence built in the county. Son Nicholas took over in 1749, bought five nearby farms to increase Waln holdings to over 1,300 acres and oversaw Walnford's greatest era of prosperity, a time when over fifty people lived and worked there. After his 1848 death, his property was divided among his wife and children. His daughter, Sarah Waln Hendrickson, oversaw the large house, a 171-acre farm and the village commercial operations.

Changes in agricultural practices and milling operations had a negative impact throughout the region. At Walnford, an 1872 fire that destroyed the gristmill underscored its decline. However, the mill was rebuilt—it is the structure one sees today—and the owners endured under falling financial circumstances that resulted in their sale of land and the contracting of debts. The younger Sarah, who died in 1907, left

A 1734 gristmill was the origin of the Walnford village and estate. This structure, the only working mill remaining in Monmouth County, was built in 1872 following the destruction of a prior mill by fire. A serene air prevails over this restful retreat.

the property to John Wilson, her longtime African American servant, which resulted in a legal contest over the will. Wilson won, compelling the family to buy back the property. Richard Waln Meirs, his wife, Anne Weightman, and son, William, transformed a reduced Walnford to a country estate. When the property was bought by Edward and Joanne Mullen in 1973, two centuries of Waln family ownership ended. The Mullens' donation of the 36-acre village core to the County of Monmouth in 1985 was expanded by the county's major acquisitions of surrounding land.

Walnford grounds became open to the public in the prerestoration era, a time that established among early visitors its reputation for peaceful serenity. An extensive restoration/preservation project was undertaken in the 1990s that culminated in the dedication of Historic Walnford at Crosswicks Creek Park on October 5, 1997. Perhaps surprisingly, Walnford's serenity has been retained over the years of public use. The restored mill grinds corn seasonally, visitors view interpretive exhibits, while a few events are held each year. Walnford is much closer to Trenton, the state capital, than Freehold, the county seat, let alone near Monmouth's more populous towns in its shore area, which likely accounts for its lesser-known existence. However, mentioned in this narrative are a number of terms that suggest a potential for an extensive broadening and extension of historic activity. Whether at an event or through a casual drop-in, Walnford's appearance enchants the visitor with a deep immersion into the past.

www.monmouthcountyparks.com; 609.259.6275
Access: Daily, 8:00 a.m.–4:30 p.m.; WOM; events. Parking: lot.

ABOUT THE AUTHOR

Photograph by William K. Heine.

Randall Gabrielan's second career as local historian overlapped his earlier corporate calling. He has written books about every section of the county and through his varied output, which includes museum exhibitions, articles, talks, slide shows, videos, tour organization and research reports, has produced more Monmouth County history than any other person ever. Gabrielan is employed by the county as executive director of its historical commission and is the appointed historian of Monmouth County and Middletown Township. His commitment to public knowledge and culture has motivated his quarter-century service as a trustee of the Middletown Township Public Library. While some may believe history is his greatest devotion, he actually loves chamber music more.

Visit us at
www.historypress.net